CW00485854

"This is a gem of a book renowned couples therap nection and couples rep understanding, wisdom, issues that divide couples, and the art and science of reconnection."

—**Melanie Greenberg, PhD**, licensed clinical psychologist, writer for *The Mindful Self-Express* blog at psychologytoday.com, and author of *The Stress-Proof Brain*

"*52 E-mails to Transform Your Marriage* is a life preserver for those struggling to create or reclaim emotional intimacy in their relationships. Couples committed to growing closer will find invaluable ideas and step-by-step guidelines to better understand each other, reconnect emotionally, and resolve conflicts that can be tough to talk about in person."

—**Andrea Bonior, PhD**, licensed clinical psychologist and author of *The Friendship Fix*

"People often tell me they are hesitant or even afraid to express their deepest needs to their spouses. And yet, self-expression is a specifically transformative ingredient that will close the emotional distance between two people. With *52 E-mails to Transform Your Marriage*, Samantha Rodman teaches how to rebuild a warm and tight connection. Engaging to read and full of insight, this book demonstrates how to break barriers and re-conjure the magic of romantic love."

> —**Jill P. Weber, PhD**, psychologist and author of
> *The Relationship Formula Workbook Series* and
> *Having Sex, Wanting Intimacy*

52 E-MAILS
to Transform Your
MARRIAGE

how to reignite intimacy &
rebuild your relationship

SAMANTHA RODMAN, PHD

New Harbinger Publications, Inc.

Publisher's Note

This publication is designed to provide accurate and authoritative information in regard to the subject matter covered. It is sold with the understanding that the publisher is not engaged in rendering psychological, financial, legal, or other professional services. If expert assistance or counseling is needed, the services of a competent professional should be sought.

Distributed in Canada by Raincoast Books

Copyright © 2016 by Samantha Rodman
New Harbinger Publications, Inc.
5674 Shattuck Avenue
Oakland, CA 94609
www.newharbinger.com

Cover design by Amy Shoup
Acquired by Jess O'Brien
Edited by Jennifer Eastman

Library of Congress Cataloging-in-Publication Data on file

18   17   16

10 9 8 7 6 5 4 3 2 1   First Printing

To my husband, with love.

Contents

Introduction

A few years into a committed relationship—and often after marriage or having kids—many couples start to feel disconnected or dissatisfied. This can feel like loneliness or like you're just not on the same page anymore. There are so many things keeping couples busy, including work, kids, housework, and social or leisure activities. Sometimes you barely have ten minutes to talk to your partner, and when you do, it's about logistics, like home repairs, finances, or who's picking up the kids from preschool.

Who Should Read This Book?

As a couples therapist, I see many couples whose relationships look great to the outside world. The partners love each other and have similar goals and values. If they have kids, they parent well, as a team. Despite these indications that they are a happy couple, however, one or both partners find themselves wondering if they even know each other anymore. They gamely schedule date nights, but these often leave both partners feeling disappointed at their lack of connection and intensity. Conversations can turn superficial and unfulfilling. There may be a platonic "roommate" dynamic or differences in sex drives that lead to resentment.

Other couples still feel connected, but they fight so frequently that they wonder if they belong together or if they would be better off apart. They are locked into unhealthy dynamics in which neither feels understood or accepted. Trust may be an issue, and discussions quickly escalate.

Still other couples have faced a tremendous stressor, like infidelity or another kind of betrayal. They are trying to get back on their feet and move forward together, but they doubt that they can ever feel loved and fully secure with each other again.

All of these types of couples—and anyone who wants to connect on a deeper level with a partner—would benefit from using this book to rekindle feelings of understanding, acceptance, and joy within their relationship. The work may be challenging, and this book is only for couples with a genuine desire to look inward and explore each partner's contribution to current relationship issues.

The exercises in this book are designed for couples who are intrinsically motivated to change in a positive way in order to create a more loving and authentic connection. If you're only going through the motions or trying to prove to your partner how wrong he or she has been about areas of conflict, this book (or any other relationship help book) will not have any significant or real effects.

Why E-mail?

E-mail is an excellent way to reconnect and to strengthen your relationship, whether it is disconnected, conflictual, ambivalent, or just lacking a spark. In-person conversations can make some people feel tongue-tied, and in some relationships, partners tend to interrupt one another in their efforts to feel heard and validated. Talking can quickly turn into fighting, especially about long-standing, sensitive topics. There is usually one partner, often the female, who longs to have deep, emotional conversations, while the other partner finds these conversations intimidating, pointless, or even harmful.

As an alternative to these frustrating discussions, e-mail correspondence can be less threatening and can allow for deeper examination of issues. Almost everyone e-mails on a regular basis, and writing an e-mail can take as much or as little time as you want. There are no passive aggressive sighs or eye rolls in an e-mail exchange, so conversations can often go deeper, since neither person feels dismissed or invalidated. And they can't escalate as rapidly as in-person conversations, which frequently end in harsh words that partners later regret.

Some readers may ask, "Why not texting or chatting?" When you text or chat, you can only type a few words or sentences before your partner feels compelled to respond. There is more pressure to respond instantaneously, particularly about emotionally charged issues. With e-mail, you can organize and express all of your thoughts without worrying about interruption or having your unedited thoughts read in real time. As any couple knows, sometimes your first expressed feelings can sound thoughtless or insensitive. If you reread your e-mail once or twice before sending, you can avoid hurting your partner by blurting something out in the heat of emotion that you may not really feel. E-mails can also put two people on an equal playing field if one is a quicker thinker or talker. After you become adept at expressing yourself in writing, you can use the communication skills you'll have learned to make your face-to-face conversations more productive and satisfying.

This book contains fifty-two e-mail assignments, spanning twelve areas that couples often find useful to discuss in order to feel closer and more connected. These e-mails will help couples, whether they've been together for months, years, or decades, to learn new things about each other and to feel more intimately bonded. Couples who feel disconnected or bitter will have learned the origin of one another's issues, which promotes empathy and understanding. Often, just knowing where your partner's personality traits or behavior patterns come from can go a long way toward feeling closer.

Why Not Therapy?

As a couples counselor, I certainly appreciate the vast benefits of in-person therapy, which can be transformative. However, very few couples are able to find an ideal situation in which they can buckle down and work on their issues with a helpful and skilled therapist. Traditional therapy has many downsides, particularly for people who are busy and do not have unlimited funds. First, clients often enter treatment in a defensive state, with years of history that they wish to share before tackling their most immediately pressing issues. Therefore, there are significant costs, in terms of both time and money, to get to the point where they can start to make any real headway in therapy.

It is also difficult to coordinate two partners' schedules (and childcare) and even harder to find a therapist that both partners click with. And then the therapist has to work reasonably close to where the couple lives or works, and, for many couples, the therapist also has to accept their health insurance. So many couples who need treatment either just don't get it or end their treatment prematurely.

This book was designed to eliminate these common complaints and obstacles. Since you dictate the pace of your efforts, you don't have to worry about spinning your wheels in treatment for months or even years. You can choose which assignments should take priority, based on your individual relationship and needs. And there are no inconveniences to your schedule, no commute to a therapist's office, no personality conflicts with a therapist, and no financial costs other than the purchase of the book. In other words, you have no excuse not to work on your relationship!

Different Ways to Use This Book

This book will be most useful if both partners write each e-mail that they choose. But that is not necessary for the book to be effective. Sometimes only one partner will want to write these e-mails, either because the other is uncomfortable with writing or because she feels that the relationship does not need work. If your partner is reluctant to e-mail, you can ask if he or she would be comfortable receiving your e-mails. Even when the e-mails go only one way, you will gain the benefit of expressing yourself, and your partner will learn more about you. And even if your partner does not want to read your e-mails (and in this case, don't send them), the e-mail prompts in this book provide an ideal tool for self-reflection in a journal and can help you clarify issues in the relationship as well as issues within yourself.

Sometimes people do not want to participate in the e-mail exercises because they are angry or unsure about remaining together; this frequently occurs after one partner has cheated or hurt the other in a major way. If you're the partner who wants to remain together, ask if you can send e-mails unilaterally. Often a betrayed or hurt partner wants to feel that the offending partner is serious about recommitting to the relationship. Writing these e-mails shows that you're willing to be vulnerable and to open yourself up to the idea of changing. After receiving a few e-mails, partners frequently warm up to the idea of participating.

You can choose to do all of the e-mails in order, from the first to the last, or you can do the chapters in the order that they most resonate with you. You can also pick just one or two e-mails to write from each chapter. If you and your partner have different ideas about how to use the book, try to compromise. Many people are not naturally prolific or quick e-mailers, but everyone can probably commit to writing at least one e-mail a week. At that rate, completing every e-mail assignment in this book would take a year. This year of e-mails would be a wonderful gift for your marriage.

If you're already in couples or individual counseling, having surmounted the obstacles to finding effective therapy that I mentioned earlier, this book can function as a way to reinvigorate the process and to get more issues on the table. As you're aware, only so much can be done in time-limited couples sessions, and both parties are often not able to fully express themselves before the time is up. E-mailing with each other between sessions is a great way to keep your momentum going, and it can bring up topics that can be explored further in session. If therapy feels like it has stalled, using this book can kick-start the process.

Additionally, many therapists do not give between-session assignments as frequently as clients would like. E-mailing between sessions can help hasten and deepen your progress. I have worked with many couples who have incorporated e-mails into their work with me, and I have found that it helps keep their therapeutic progress moving forward and increases intimacy between sessions.

If you see an individual therapist, it would be helpful to discuss these e-mails in your sessions. Writing can help clarify your own thoughts, feelings, needs, and desires. Your therapist can support and guide you through communicating openly and honestly with your partner and can also help you process e-mails that you receive.

Be Nice

Your e-mail correspondence will end quickly if you and your partner use these e-mails to attack or hurt one another. You should not include sarcasm, attacks, or harsh criticism. These e-mails are about you and your feelings, not your analysis of your partner's shortcomings. Take your e-mails seriously, which means limit your jokes and make yourself vulnerable by being as honest and self-aware as you can. Try to cultivate a mindset of openness to feedback and putting your shy or embarrassed self to the side. Also, the e-mails you receive will be honest, so commit to welcoming this honesty and do not punish your partner for it. Make sure that your own honesty comes from a collaborative and well-intentioned place.

Try to use "I" statements, such as "I feel lonely when we don't talk during the workday," rather than accusatory "you" statements, like, "You never call me during the day." Think of each e-mail as a bid for connection, a small entreaty from your partner to pay attention to something important to him. Responding with kindness to a partner's bids for affection is one of the secrets to a happy marriage, according to research by John Gottman.[1] Even if your partner's e-mail doesn't seem to include many deep issues (from your perspective), it was likely difficult to write what he or she did. Empathize with your partner and be validating when reading and responding to e-mails. This doesn't mean you have to say that you feel the same way your partner does, only that your partner's feelings make sense to you—that you can see where your partner stands.

The Specifics of E-mailing

Although you get specific directions in each chapter with prompts for writing your e-mails, there are some tips to keep in mind.

First, make sure that one partner doesn't end up nagging the other to participate. There should be one designated day each week for partners to e-mail one another. Both of you can read the e-mail assignment and copy it down (or take a picture of it on your phone), and you should write each other at approximately the same time, so one partner's e-mail doesn't turn into a response.

Each e-mail should end with two or three open-ended questions that were sparked by the assignment. Open-ended questions can't be answered with just yes or no, and you'll see many examples of this in the sample e-mails below. (If you receive a yes-or-no question, however, try to respond to it in depth.) Partners should respond to these questions later that day or the next day. This way, neither partner is left wondering and worrying about the other's reaction. It would be good to schedule a half hour to write a focused e-mail, but don't worry if it initially takes you a lot longer. If you need to, set a limit that is reasonable and send what you've written within that time frame.

Many people will find the information their partner shares with them so interesting that they will want to keep the correspondence going by e-mailing on the same topic after the initial question and the follow-up response. But don't be disappointed if your partner doesn't want to continue on one topic, especially at first. Remember, many people have never written anything like these e-mails. It may feel at first like you're writing in a foreign language, in which emotional disclosure supersedes the usual chitchat and banter. This can be difficult, and all of your emotional energy may be expended in the e-mail itself and the response, without any left for additional discussions about the topic.

In each e-mail, the first prompt is about how you feel writing about the subject. This is an important way to clarify your feelings, and it gives your partner a window into your mind and heart. I usually ask you to use at least three prompts in addition to the first. You'll get more out of this book if you use more prompts than that. But if writing e-mails is completely outside of your comfort zone, you can stick with four prompts at first and try to increase it over time. The prompts and example e-mails can be viewed as inspiration rather than strict assignments, since the goal of this book is to help your unique relationship, and no two relationships are identical. Tweak the questions or prompts to fit your own situation. Lastly, include a closing that makes you feel connected and affirms your connection, like "I love you," or "Thank you for reading this."

The example e-mails are fictionalized, and any resemblance to real people is coincidental. However, the thoughts and feelings in the examples are based upon issues that I have encountered in my practice. Gender pronouns will be alternated for ease of reading, but most issues discussed can apply to both genders and to individuals of any sexual orientation.

Sometimes I will say "husband" and "wife," although the same dynamics are at play in unmarried relationships.

Many e-mails will include personal content, so keep this in mind if you're using your work e-mail address. You may also want to dedicate a special folder or label for these messages. And, of course, don't delete them! You will most likely cherish many of them and want to reread them later on.

Now, let's get started!

CHAPTER 1

When Our Story Started

Many people reading this book are feeling disappointed, disconnected, sad, angry, or all of the above. However, if you start your e-mail correspondence by focusing on the negative, it is unlikely to go well. Start on a positive note, reminiscing about earlier, happier stages in your relationship and expressing admiration and appreciation for your partner. Emphasizing the good, even if it feels unnatural right now, will lay the groundwork for you to open up to the process of e-mailing.

1   When I First Met You…

Here, you have a chance to share all the wonderful things that you thought during your first encounter with your partner. This will start your e-mailing off on the right foot, so try to dig deep and come up with specific memories. It is helpful to reminisce lovingly about the traits that originally drew you to your partner, particularly if you've recently felt disillusioned or filled with despair.

Use the first prompt, as well as at least three others, and end with two or three open-ended questions!

- Discussing how we first met makes me feel _____.

- My first thought about you was: _____.

- Here's what I thought about your looks or personality or voice or clothes: _____.

- I realized I wanted to date you when _____.

- Here are some specific things that attracted me to you: _____.

- Here's what I thought about the likelihood of us ending up together: _____.

- Here's what I told other people about you: _____.

- After we first spoke, I felt _____.

Dear Ellen,

I'm feeling positive about writing you this e-mail. Maybe it can be a nice part of our day—to read these things about each other. When I first met you, I thought, *Whoa.* I didn't expect James to know any girls, so I wasn't really looking forward to the party. Then you walked in, and I thought, *That is a girl that I want to know better.* I realized I wanted to date you after our first conversation, when you said you thought I was funny. I was shocked that you thought my jokes were funny and not dumb! I was also attracted to your smile, your eyes, and of course, your body.

My questions:

- What attracted you to me?

- Do you still think I'm funny?

- Did you want to date me right away, or was it only after we talked on the phone?

I love you, honey,

Mark

Dear Mark,

I feel ambivalent about writing you this e-mail. As you know, I am not feeling close or connected lately, and I don't usually think about our early dating life when I am feeling upset. But here goes...

I first thought you were tall and cute, in a dorky way. I thought you were funny and smart and not like the usual meatheads I went for in high school. I told my friends that I met a genuinely nice guy who liked math and science, and they were surprised. Rachel said, "Maybe you're growing up." That was the first time I thought about us dating seriously.

Questions:

- Did you like my personality at first or just my boobs?

- When did you first think we would date seriously?

Love,

Ellen

2 When I First Loved You

Now you will build upon your first e-mail and discuss the moment or moments when you knew that you wanted to commit to your partner. Most couples, especially those who aren't feeling connected, don't revisit this early, honeymoon phase of their relationship. This is unfortunate, since reminiscing about these days can rekindle feelings of closeness.

Use the first prompt, as well as at least three others, and end with two or three open-ended questions!

- When discussing when I first knew I loved you, I feel _____.

- I first remember thinking I loved you when _____.

- I first wanted to tell you I loved you when _____.

- When I told you that I loved you (or when you told me that you loved me) for the first time, I felt _____.

- When we decided to be in a committed relationship, I felt _____.

- When I think back to the early days of being in love with you, I feel _____.

- A special memory that I have from those days is _____.

- I never told you this thought or feeling from those days:_____.

- A song that reminds me of those days is _____.

- Three things I loved about you from the beginning are _____.

Dear Yana,

I feel warm and happy writing to you about when I first knew I loved you. I have never felt as good as I did in those first months, before we found out you were pregnant and things got stressful. I first wanted to tell you that I loved you in Miami, but I decided that it would seem too fast. Then, when I told you at your mom's house, and you said it back, I felt awesome. I felt like the luckiest guy in the world.

A special memory I have is of us making out in the bar on our first date and thinking that all the other guys were jealous that I scored such a hot girl.

Questions:

· When did you know you loved me?

· Do you remember making out with me that night?

· What did you think when I told you I loved you?

Love,

Michael

Hi Michael,

I feel both sad and happy about writing you this e-mail, because when I think about first being in love, I can't help thinking about the baby. I knew I loved you the first time we met, when you told me that you bought your nephew a rock lullaby CD. I thought, *This is the kind of guy I could marry.* I've never told you this, but that was the only time that I had ever that thought about any of my boyfriends.

The song that reminds me of us dating is "Float On." When you told me you loved me, I felt so happy. The first thing I thought was, *I'm glad I didn't say it when I first wanted to, because now I know he really means it.*

I want to ask you:

- When did you first want to tell me you loved me?

- Did you consider leaving when I got pregnant?

- How did you feel when we lost the baby?

XO,

Yana

3 Moving In Together

Moving in together is a tremendous step in any relationship. This stage can be rife with arguments and misunderstandings, but it is also often filled with passion, particularly if couples move in together during their "honeymoon" or infatuation stage. Living together allows you to see your partner in a new way, and your dynamic often changes. Here is an opportunity to either reminisce about your earliest days sharing a home or to discuss the idea of living together in the future.

Use the first prompt, as well as at least three others, and end with two or three open-ended questions!

- E-mailing you about living together makes me feel _____.

- When we first moved in together, I felt _____.

- I was surprised to learn that you _____.

- I had to learn these skills in order to live with you: _____.

- This is how my upbringing shaped my ideas about living together: _____.

- Here is how I feel about the idea of living together: _____.

- This is how I feel about the connection between love and living together: _____.

- When we consider living together in the future, I feel _____.

- I think I would be good (or not good) at living together, because _____.

- I feel ready (or not ready) to move in together, because _____.

- Here is how I feel about staying in a relationship but choosing to live separately: _____.

Dear Fiona,

I am anxious about this e-mail, because it's such a sore subject. I love you very much, but I am really leery about the idea of sharing my space. This is a tough time for me in school, and exams are kicking my butt. It makes me anxious to think about you moving in and then feeling lonely and abandoned when I spend most of my time in the hospital and the library.

I am a very weird person, and I have weird habits. I don't want to ruin what we have now by rushing to move in together. Further down the road, when we can afford a bigger place—and when I'm out of school and have a more regular schedule—I will be less hesitant. But you know my feelings about marriage, and living together seems like a short step away from that. I love you very much, and I think our love can thrive even more when we don't share an apartment. I am sorry to keep disappointing you.

Questions:

- Can you wait another eighteen months before we revisit this topic?

- Are you really okay with not getting married or is that something you say because you think I'll change my mind?

Your weirdo,

Caleb

Dear Caleb,

This topic makes me really sad. We have talked it to death, but I feel like you don't hear me. To me, being in love means sleeping together every night, sharing a space, cooking together—all of that. My friends are all dating guys in high-pressure jobs, and med school is the same deal, except that you have more overnights. I would not be sitting around, wasting away, while you were in class. I wouldn't be resenting you. If there is anything I resent, it is the caricature of some bereft, pathetic girlfriend texting you that your dinner is getting cold.

You say you would be tough to live with, but we virtually live together now, except we pay two rents. I can't envision a future together if, after three years, we still aren't living together. From the time I was twelve, when I saw Marisa and Clark move in together, I was looking forward to living with my boyfriend one day. I do *not* want to get married, but I do want a partner, and to me, that means making a home together.

My questions:

- When will you be ready to talk about this more seriously?

- Would you be open to going to a couples counselor if we can't resolve this issue on our own?

I love you,

Fiona

4 ♥ Love and Marriage

In early marriage, newlyweds often experience a honeymoon phase in which everything seems rosy and perfect. But in a couple of years—or when a baby is born—couples often enter a disillusionment phase, colored by disappointment with each other and doubt about whether they are meant to be together. If couples weather this stage, they can move into an acceptance phase, during which they learn to accept one another on a deep level and are aware of their personal contribution to any recurring marital issues.

The marriage that you saw growing up affects your current views on marriage and your default mode of interaction with your partner. If you saw a disconnected or conflicted marriage, you may think of marriage as a surefire way to kill passion and connection. For example, adult children of divorce are frequently wary of marriage, as they experienced the effects of marital dissolution firsthand. People are also likely to unconsciously and automatically respond to partners in the ways that their parents responded to one another. In this exercise, you'll share your thoughts and feelings about marriage, and help your partner understand the link between your background and your current perspective.

Use the first prompt, as well as at least three others, and end with two or three open-ended questions!

- Here is how I feel e-mailing you about marriage: _____.

- Here is what I learned about marriage from observing my parents: _____.

- When you (or I) proposed, or decided to get married, I felt _____.

- Planning the wedding made (or makes) me feel _____.

- On our wedding day (or honeymoon), I felt _____.

- Here is the phase I think we're in now (honeymoon, disillusionment, or acceptance): _____.

- I think our honeymoon phase lasted until _____.

- Here is what I think about the disillusionment phase: _____.

- Here is what I think about the acceptance phase: _____.

- My favorite memory from our early marriage (or our whole marriage) is _____.

- One issue that we have really conquered together in our marriage is _____.

- This is how I feel about the connection between love and marriage: _____.

Dear Kevin,

I feel unhappy writing this e-mail to you because it has made me realize that we're in the disillusionment phase. That must be what I've been feeling for the past year. When you proposed to me, I was on top of the world, and I loved planning the wedding. The first year went really well, and my best memory is just cuddling on the couch watching *Mad Men*.

I think that things started to go downhill when I stopped working. You supported my decision, but I think you secretly resented it, because, in reality, we thought I would get pregnant right away. Now I'm just this weird stay-at-home-wife person. Like *Mad Men*, actually.

I feel like we need to get to the acceptance phase, or things will just get worse. I have to figure out what to do if we don't get pregnant soon. I wish there were more part-time options. Also, I wish you'd be honest with me about your feelings, instead of making little remarks here and there.

Questions:

- If you could pick any career or school or life path for me, what would you choose?

- Do you resent me for leaving work?

I love you, and I want to get back to where we were last year. I think it's possible, and I hope you agree.

Love,

Erin

Dear Erin,

I am anxious about writing you this e-mail, because I am anxious about every conversation or e-mail we have nowadays. You always think that I'm out to get you or that I'm making fun of you.

I loved our honeymoon; it was the happiest time in my life, not to mention the best sex. You looked so beautiful in your bikini, and I loved parasailing and windsurfing with you. I thought we were going to break the mold and have a really happy, egalitarian marriage—best friends and also passionately in love. That is what I never saw when I was a kid, and I thought it was a myth till I met you.

I think we are in the disillusionment phase now. You seem repulsed when I touch you, unless you're ovulating, and then it's all about conceiving. I want a baby too, but I still also feel desire for you, whereas you don't seem to feel any for me. I hope you want to recapture our connection as much as I do.

Questions:

- Do you enjoy sex with me anymore?
- Are we going to take a break from trying to conceive if it doesn't happen soon?
- Do you like writing these e-mails?

I love you, baby,

Kevin

CHAPTER 2

Who I Am

You need to answer certain questions about yourself in order to build a satisfying and authentic life. These questions about priorities, identity, and values become particularly salient when individuals experience life transitions, such as getting married, having a baby, dealing with the death of a loved one, or starting a new job.

In this set of e-mails, you'll have the opportunity to discuss personal, existential issues with your partner. Your partner will get a deeper look into who you are and who you want to be, which can be a relationship-changing experience, particularly if you haven't discussed these issues in a long time.

5 Am I Fulfilled?

Neither you nor your partner is a static entity. Both of you are constantly growing and changing. Women often think that men are less introspective and focused on self-development, but this is untrue. Men frequently focus on self-development in different ways, like career growth and physical and health-related changes, rather than in-depth introspection about emotional issues. Here, you can discuss whether you feel fulfilled in different areas of your life, and you can explore how these feelings impact your relationship.

Use the first prompt, as well as at least three others, and end with two or three open-ended questions!

- Writing this e-mail, I feel _____.

- I often think about whether I am fulfilled in this aspect of my life: _____.

- I feel fulfilled (or unfulfilled) spiritually, because _____.

- I feel fulfilled (or unfulfilled) in my career, because _____.

- I feel fulfilled (or unfulfilled) emotionally, because _____.

- My life is different from how I thought it would be when I was a child. I thought it would be _____, and I feel _____ about it.

- When I feel (or don't feel) fulfilled in my life, this is how it impacts our relationship: _____.

- Over time, I have grown more fulfilled in this area of my life: _____ and less fulfilled in this area: _____.

Dear Leslie,

It's hard for me to write about this stuff, because it hits so close to home. I am increasingly realizing that I'm not fulfilled. As a kid, I never thought I would be working for someone else, and I pictured having my own store, like Dad. But when I was offered the restaurant job, I just took it and didn't look back, until now.

I think constantly about whether I should start my own business. Right now I have a good paycheck and predictable hours. A new business would give me neither of those at first, but it would be something of my own. It would be much more fulfilling, but I'm terrified about the possibility of quitting a stable job and then failing when I'm on my own.

Questions:

- Do you think I should stay or go? Tell me what you really think, not what you think I want to hear.

- Are you still happy staying at home? I've noticed you talk a lot about being bored lately.

Love,

Adam

Dear Adam,

This e-mail comes at a good time. I have been thinking about whether I am fulfilled in our current setup. I am feeling less than happy as a stay-at-home mom now that Lacy is in school. I have thought about a few options, like getting more involved in the church, especially the preschool, or being a yoga instructor, or getting more invested in the PTA.

When I am dissatisfied with my life in this way, it impacts our marriage. Sometimes I even resent that you get to go out and interact with adults at the restaurant. I want to figure out what to do with my life before my dissatisfaction turns into depression.

Questions:

- What do you think I should do?
- Will you be disappointed if I choose to remain home or take an unpaid position?

Yours,

Leslie

6 The Lifestyle I'd Like To Have with You

Your family upbringing and your peers, schools, and jobs can all impact the lifestyle that you want. Partners often disagree on the importance of money, how to manage finances, where to live, and how much emphasis to place on career versus family. In this e-mail, you can discuss the type of lifestyle that you aspire to and why. Hopefully, it will help your partner to hear you and empathize with you in a new way.

Use the first prompt, as well as at least three others, and end with two or three open-ended questions!

- Writing this e-mail to you I feel _____.

- When I was growing up, here's how money was managed: _____.

- Growing up, I felt I had less (or more, the same amount of) money as my peers, and this made me feel _____.

- The income that would make me feel financially secure is _____.

- I think the ideal balance between time spent earning money versus time spent with our family is _____.

- Here is how I feel about one of us being a stay-at-home parent: _____.

- The type of neighborhood I want to live in is _____.

- I think we should move out of our current home, because _____.

- Historically, I have found it hard to empathize with your thoughts on money or lifestyle, because _____.

Dear Charles,

I feel nervous writing you this e-mail, because these issues have led to fights in the past. But maybe this will help give you a different perspective. Growing up, my dad drank away our money, and my mom had to make do with basically only her little salary and my grandparents' help. I resolved never to be irresponsible with money and to always have a financial cushion. But I also missed my mom a lot when she worked, especially when I was in grade school, so I wanted to be home for my own kids.

If we have savings, which we do, and if I am home with the kids, I have all that I need. Spending a lot of money on cars or vacations makes me anxious, and, to be honest, I don't enjoy things if I picture them sucking our savings dry. I know you think I'm boring and a Nervous Nellie, but it is very hard for me to change, given my background.

Questions:

- Earlier in our relationship, you said you liked that I was frugal. When did it change?

- Do you think the children really get made fun of for our car, or did you just say that to hurt me?

Love,

Cheryl

Dear Cheryl,

This topic irritates me, because I feel that you are unnecessarily stingy. I feel embarrassed in front of the guys at work when I say we never travel and, of course, when they see my car. You act like I am materialistic, but we have boys, and I know what boys like. They like nice cars and Wii systems and cool gadgets. I never had that stuff, and now I am in a position to give it to my kids, but you're thwarting me at every turn.

I know you want to be home with the boys, but they are in school now. It is completely feasible for you to work part-time at the clinic again, and that extra money might make you feel more secure. If not, I am fine with how much we have, and I'm sure I'll get a raise next year. I wish you could understand my perspective. You can't take it with you, and I want to give the kids—and us—a great life.

Questions:

- Would you feel better if you started bringing in some more money?

- When your friends get new cars, why don't you seem angry with them for being materialistic, but you do with me?

Love,

Charles

♥7 What I'm Working on Changing

There are many things that people want to improve or change in themselves, including habits, lifestyles, parenting practices, and interpersonal style. We often do not share these aspirations or goals with our partners, which is unfortunate, because conversations about vulnerable, personal issues have the potential to make couples feel newly connected. Also, if you know what your partner wants to change, not only can you can be supportive and understanding, but you may even be inspired to change in similar ways yourself.

Use the first prompt, as well as at least three others, and end with two or three open-ended questions!

- When writing this e-mail, I feel _____.

- Here are three ways in which I am trying to change as a person: _____.

- The area in which I would most like to change is _____.

- I have been thinking about changing in this way: _____ ever since _____.

- The catalyst for my desire to change was _____.

- If I could change in these ways, I would feel _____.

- I am confident (or anxious) about my ability to change because _____.

- To help me change in these ways, you could _____.

- Thinking back on my childhood, I think these potential changes are important to me because _____.

- If I changed in this way: _____, it would affect our relationship, because _____.

Dear Leah,

I feel confident writing this e-mail, because I've given these issues a lot of thought, and I've made some important resolutions. I want to eat healthier, quit smoking, and be more active. I have been thinking about this since the baby was born. I want to be there for her longer than my dad was there for me. I am anxious about my ability to stick to a weight-loss program, because I've failed before, but I never had as big a motivator as this before.

You could help me by having sex with me whenever I skip dessert. Just kidding (not really). You could also not buy ice cream or candy, and you could go running with me.

My questions:

- Do you want to start this effort together?
- Do you think I can lose fifty pounds by the summer?

I love you, sweetheart,

Greg

Dear Greg,

I have thought a lot about this e-mail, which is why it's late (sorry!). Since the baby came, I have been thinking a lot about my mom and the ways that she could have made my life easier. I was a shy kid, and it was worse because my mom never joined the PTA or made friends with my classmates' moms, so I didn't have a lot of playdates. I am an introvert like her, but I want to commit to making friends for us as a family. I don't want Ella's life to be just school, aftercare, and hanging out with you and me.

You could help me with this by reaching out to the people at work, since I know many of them have kids too. Also, you could be positive about people instead of finding things wrong with them.

Questions:

- Did your family have people over a lot?

- Who was your closest family friend?

- Do you think Ella would thrive more in a different neighborhood, one with more kids?

Love,

Leah

8 Introvert or Extrovert?

Many couples find it interesting to discuss where each partner falls on the extraversion and introversion spectrum. Extroverts are social and derive their energy and happiness from interacting with others. They don't need much alone time and consider it relaxing to engage with other people. Introverts find group interactions to be generally stressful and prefer to spend downtime alone or with a partner or best friend. Introverts with kids can become much more overwhelmed than extroverted parents; introverts can feel like they can never escape from a group, even in their homes.

When two introverts or two extroverts are in a relationship, it can be easy for them to decide on common activities, how much to socialize, what types of vacations to take, and how to parent. In extrovert-introvert pairings, however, extroverts can become frustrated with their partners' need for time alone, and introverts can become overwhelmed trying to keep up with their partners' need to socialize. After the honeymoon phase, introverted partners may be considered boring by their partners, while extroverts may be thought to be shallow.

Use the first prompt, as well as at least three others, and end with two or three open-ended questions!

- Writing to you about this topic, I feel _____.

- I think I am an extrovert (or introvert, or in the middle), because I enjoy _____.

- My parents were introverts (or extroverts), and this affected me by _____.

- Here are three things I like (or don't like) about being an extrovert (or introvert): _____.

- I think you are an extrovert (or introvert), because you enjoy _____.

- Here is how we complement each other: _____.

- Here is how our pairing leads to issues: _____.

- Here are ways we could compromise if we are in an extrovert-introvert relationship: _____.

Dear Barbara,

I feel amused writing to you about this topic, because I think
we finally have one in the bag. I think we are both introverts,
which is probably why we picked this book instead of going to
sit with a therapist face-to-face! Three things I like about being
an introvert are: I think deeply about issues, I am able to pursue
hobbies on my own, and I don't become anxious if you have to
travel for work, leaving me home alone.

On the other hand, I dislike feeling uncomfortable at work
events and feeling awkward when neighbors chat with me. Also,
I regret that I wasn't able to be as outgoing as our girls would
have liked.

You and I complement each other because we are so similar.
I tried to date more outgoing women in college, and it never felt
right. I am glad we are birds of a feather.

Questions:

- Do you consider yourself entirely an introvert or more
  in the middle of the spectrum?

- Did you ever date an extrovert?

All my love,

Victor

Dear Victor,

I am sad writing about this topic, because I feel that, over time, we have grown apart. As I have gotten older—and with the help of therapy and Prozac—I have started to come out of my shell. I have tried to share this insight with you, but I think you don't want to hear me. You are a definite introvert, but I think I was always just socially anxious. Now I see that I do enjoy socializing.

I have wished for years now that you were more open to getting together with other couples, even just the Booths or the Klonskys, whom we have known forever but have never even had over for dinner. I know it might seem awkward to invite them after all this time, but I would enjoy it.

I like that you are a quiet guy, and still waters run deep. But I think I have changed somewhat, and I would love if you would try to accept and even appreciate this.

Questions:

- What type of socializing would be easiest for you, if you had to pick something?

- How much would you dislike having people over for dinner?

Love,

Barbara

9 My Issues with Mental Health

People often think that their partners know much more about their individual struggles with mood, anxiety, eating, addiction, and childhood issues than they really do. These are sensitive topics, but if you are affected by them, it can be a relief to finally discuss this aspect of your life in depth with your partner. When your partner shares this e-mail with you, try to be particularly validating and reassuring in your response, as it is tough to talk about these issues.

Use the first prompt, as well as at least three others, and end with two or three open-ended questions!

- Writing this e-mail, I feel _____.

- The mental health issues I struggle with are _____.

- Here is how I have been affected by the following issue or issues: _____.

  - depression

  - stress

  - anxiety

  - bipolar disorder

  - ADHD

  - addiction

  - trauma

- dysfunctional family relationships
- verbal, sexual, physical, or emotional abuse
- body-image issues
- any other relevant issue
- I want (or do not want) to see a therapist or psychiatrist or attend a support group for my issues, because _____.
- You can support my struggles best by _____.
- I appreciate how you support me in these ways: _____.

Dear Eliza,

I don't know how to write this e-mail to you, since I don't think I struggle with any mental health issues. But I figure I can write about my jackass brother. Pete was pretty terrible to me, from before I can remember until he moved out. I don't think you understand the extent of it. Suffice it to say, if our kids ever treated each other or anyone else the way Pete treated me, I would ground them forever.

Pete was a bully, and he still is, but now he does it at work and to Pam. My parents didn't understand that he was really beating the crap out of me on a regular basis. They thought we were just playing. Mom had her head in the clouds, and Dad was so messed up from combat that he was barely there.

You can support me by not asking me to hang out with Pete. Our kids can have your sister's kids as cousins. Every time I see him, I feel sick. He is still the same arrogant ass, but it's even worse now, because he pretends he likes me.

Questions:

- Did you ever get bullied by your sister?

- Do you think I have any other mental issues I'm not thinking of?

> Your loving husband,
>
> Jim

Dear Jim,

This is a hard e-mail to write, because I am resolving to share something I have actually never told you. In fact, I have never told anyone this. I think I am bulimic. When I eat too much, if I am stressed out, I make myself throw up. I do it a lot sometimes, and then for months I won't. Sometimes you ask where certain foods are in the fridge or cabinet, and I say I don't know, but I do know: I have eaten it and thrown it up. I hope you don't feel disgusted.

Recently, Jasmine has been asking me if I think she's fat. She is the same age I was when I started doing this, and I am terrified that it's genetic or that I have messed her up by always being on a diet. I have been reading some books about healthy eating and body acceptance, and I think I am going to start seeing a therapist.

Questions:

- Do you think I am crazy?
- Do you think I have messed up Jasmine?

Love,

Eliza

CHAPTER 3

How Do I Give and Receive Love?

Everyone has different ideas of the perfect way to express love. When partners enjoy expressing and receiving love in the same ways, their relationships go smoothly. However, when partners value different expressions of commitment and connection, this can lead to misunderstandings, distance, and resentment.

Here, we'll explore your and your partner's love-giving styles. If you understand what makes each of you feel loved and connected, you can respond to each other in a way that will leave you both feeling fulfilled.

10 Love Languages

Gary Chapman's book *The 5 Love Languages: The Secret to Love That Lasts* discusses how people express love and want to receive love in very different ways.[2] These "love languages" are based on your temperament, as well as how love was expressed in your family when you were growing up. The five love languages that Chapman discusses are

- *quality time*—spending a day together, just hanging out and talking;

- *words of affirmation*—telling your partner, "I really appreciate your taking a day off work when I was sick, you're a great husband";

- *acts of service*—taking the car to be washed, doing the dishes;

- *receiving gifts*—whether something big, like jewelry, or something small, like a new mug; and

- *physical touch*—sex, hugging, holding hands, kissing, massaging, or anything else.

In my practice, I see more males than females who say that physical touch is their love language, and more females than males who like receiving gifts or acts of service. Equal numbers of both genders seem to value quality time and words of affirmation. People can have more than one love language, but often there are one or two top ones. You can take a love languages quiz on Gary Chapman's website (http://www.5love languages.com), but many people know theirs just from reading the categories. As you can imagine, conflicts arise when people express love in the language they themselves value, rather than the language that their partners value.

Use the first prompt, as well as at least three others, and end with two or three open-ended questions!

- Discussing love languages with you makes me feel _____.

- From reading the list, I think my (or your) top two love language are _____.

- My love languages were shaped by how I grew up in this way: _____.

- When we first met, here is how you responded to my love languages: _____.

- One love language we may have in common is _____.

- The best way that you address my love languages is _____.

- If you focused more on my love languages, I would feel _____.

- I try to address your love languages by _____.

- Here are ways we can try to keep each other's love languages in mind: _____.

Dear Peter,

I am excited to discuss love languages with you, because it's a concept that I am really on board with. My top two love languages are physical touch (no shock there) and words of affirmation. The best way that you address my love languages is by complimenting me, including my looks and my sense of humor. I do wish that you were more enthusiastic about casual affectionate touching. Our sex life is great, but I wish that we also touched in a nonsexual way.

I think your love languages are acts of service and gifts, and I try to give you both, although lately I have been slacking on the gifts front. But your birthday is coming up . . .

My questions:

- Are you annoyed when I try to touch you throughout the day?

- What acts of service could I do for you that I don't do?

I love you,

Matt

Dear Matt,

I feel frustrated writing this, since it's a bit of a sore subject for me. My number one love language is acts of service, and I have tried to tell you over the years that it is really important to me when you do what you say you're going to do. For me, if you say that you're going to take Trixie to the vet, it is really important that you follow through.

I think that acts of service are my love language because my dad never followed through with anything. He didn't even take out the trash like the other dads, and I did it as soon as I was big enough, but I resented that all he seemed to do for us was bring home a paycheck (sometimes).

When you and I first met, you were all about acts of service, and I found that really reassuring. Now I feel like you don't appreciate how difficult it is for me to run the household, particularly when you travel. If you helped out more, I would feel a lot closer, and I would probably be more physically affectionate.

Love,

Peter

♥11 Little Ways to Show You Care

On my website, http://www.drpsychmom.com, I wrote the following list of one hundred little ways to feel connected with your partner. Glance through the list and think of which ones are relevant to your and your partner's love languages. You can also print this list from http://www.newharbinger/34602.com.

1. Send your partner an e-card.

2. When you're filling up your car with gas, run into the mini-mart and buy your partner his favorite snack.

3. Pack your partner's lunch.

4. Put a note in your partner's bag or coat pocket.

5. Clean your partner's car.

6. Initiate sex.

7. Find a movie that your partner would really like and watch it together.

8. Compliment your partner in front of other people.

9. E-mail your partner a happy memory of your life together.

10. Get a picture of you and your partner framed for her desk or nightstand.

11. E-mail your partner a cute selfie.

12. Call or visit someone your partner wishes you were closer to, such as one of their parents.

13. Tell your partner about the nicest thing they did for you today.

14. French kiss your partner.

15. Bring your partner a special drink from a coffee shop.

16. Bake something for your partner.

17. Buy your partner a bottle of champagne to celebrate a random anniversary (like the day you moved into your house or the day you bought your dog).

18. Draw your partner a funny stick-figure picture of the two of you.

19. Write your partner a list of her most attractive qualities.

20. Save the last piece of dessert for your partner, instead of giving it to the kids.

21. Take a walk together.

22. Play your wedding song or a song that is meaningful to both of you.

23. Shower together.

24. Decide to learn more about something your partner is interested in.

25. Book a babysitter and go on a date night, as a surprise.

26. Research new restaurants that your partner would like.

27. Make your partner a hot breakfast.

28. Give your partner a big hug.

29. Go in late to work and get coffee with your partner at a cafe.

30. Come home during naptime, if your partner stays home with the kids, just to hang out together.

31. Hang a banner to welcome your partner home, even just from work.

32. Write a status update on social media about how great your partner is.

33. Find a picture from when you and your partner first met, and leave it where she can find it as a surprise.

34. Buy new clothes for yourself that you know your partner would like to see you wear.

35. Buy new clothes for your partner that are in the style he likes (not what you want him to like).

36. Buy or make your partner a heart-shaped cookie.

37. When the kids are being loud and annoying, intercept them so your partner can relax.

38. Share a sexual fantasy with your partner via text.

39. Plan a childlike activity with your partner, like a corn maze or a zoo.

40. Buy your partner a few lottery tickets.

41. Send your partner a letter through the mail.

42. Give your partner a massage.

43. Make the bed the way your partner prefers it.

44. Leave a Post-it on your partner's computer, saying something nice.

45. Tell your partner why you are lucky to have him.

46. Let your partner pick the television show.

47. Sing a song into your partner's voice mail.

48. Have the kids draw a picture for your partner.

49. Serve your partner first at dinner.

50. Tell your partner a way that knowing him has improved you as a person.

51. Message your partner a cheesy joke that will make her laugh.

52. Ask what your partner's favorite meal is, and then make it.

53. Notice if your partner has a belonging that is wearing out, like a pair of gloves, a hat, or a bag, and buy her a new one.

54. Dance around the living room with your partner.

55. Ask your partner how she always deals so well with a certain situation that always overwhelms you.

56. Ask your partner to teach you something that he knows and you don't, such as how to cook a certain dish or how to ski.

57. Do a striptease for your partner.

58. Find and display a sweet childhood photo of your partner.

59. Research places to take a couples' vacation.

60. Research places to retire, and send her the links to check them out.

61. Approach your partner in a public place as though he were an attractive stranger.

62. Buy your partner perfume or cologne.

63. Surprise your partner at work with a food delivery for lunch.

64. Ask your partner to play a board game.

65. Put a Hershey's kiss in your partner's lunch.

66. Write a haiku for your partner.

67. Make an appointment for a massage for your partner.

68. Arrange with your partner a secret code word that means "I want to have sex tonight." Use in public.

69. Initiate a sexual act that you don't usually do!

70. Get your partner a book that she might like.

71. Paint pottery together.

72. Take a trial lesson in ballroom dancing.

73. Go bowling.

74. Bring home a few bottles of wine and create a wine tasting for your partner.

75. Clean the refrigerator for your partner.

76. Donate some of your things to clear out more space for your partner in the closet.

77. Send your partner a video or mp3 of a romantic song.

78. Send your partner a picture of a cute animal.

79. Plan a day out for you and your partner a few weeks or months in advance, something you can look forward to.

80. Replace your partner's toothbrush.

81. Get your partner a mug that says World's Best Husband or Wife or Boyfriend or Girlfriend.

82. Tell your partner that you were talking with your coworkers, and you realized you have the best partner of any of them.

83. Tally up the number of times you think about your partner during the day and present her with the piece of paper later.

84. In normal conversation, call your partner "my beautiful wife" (or "my handsome husband," or "boyfriend" or "girlfriend," as the case may be).

85. Do a craft project with your partner.

86. Have a date night at home with candles, wine, and cheese and crackers after the kids go to bed.

87. If you're not the partner who cares the most about household tasks, say, "I want to do whatever project you want me to do tonight. Just tell me what to do, and I'll do it."

88. Write down five things you thought about your partner when you were first getting to know him, and leave this as a surprise note.

89. Buy your partner whatever you were going to get her for Christmas on some random day instead. Then get something else for Christmas, even if it's small.

90. Try out a new sex toy.

91. Deal with your partner's dry cleaning, or do another task she finds annoying.

92. Compliment your partner on something that isn't physical.

93. Compliment your partner on something that is physical.

94. Make hot chocolate for your partner.

95. Learn how to make your partner's favorite mixed drink.

96. Research your partner's astrological sign and send her your thoughts about it.

97. Learn how to say, "I want to sleep with you" in a different language, and say it to your partner.

98. Buy your partner whatever candy he liked most as a kid.

99. Exercise with your partner.

100. Kiss your partner ten times today.

After leading with how you feel writing this e-mail to your partner, state five things from this list that you wish she would do for you and five things that you would consider doing for your partner that would require pushing yourself outside your comfort zone. If you're very averse to doing the things mentioned, then you don't have to do them, but learning what would be valuable to your partner is important in and of itself. In chapter 11 you'll have an opportunity to commit to changing in a few small ways for your partner, so remember this list when you get there!

Dear Elizabeth,

I like writing you this e-mail, because I think some of these things would be really great for our relationship. I am also curious what you most wish for. My top five things that I want you to do for me are:

1. plan a day out for us;

2. try a new sex toy;

3. go running with me;

4. initiate sex; and

5. share a sexual fantasy with me via text.

As you can see, mine have the theme of physical touch, but I also just want to spend time with you. Here are the ones I would be pushing myself outside my comfort zone to do for you.

1. scrapbook with you

2. yoga with you

3. write you a haiku

4. ballroom-dancing lessons (but I don't actually know if you'd like this or not)

5. paint pottery with you

But I am willing to do some of those if you do some of mine!

Love,

Joseph

Dear Joseph,

I'm excited to write this to you, because I want to make you scrapbook with me! Ha ha! But I think that we definitely should do more things together aside from watching TV. I am also looking forward to seeing if you do some of my favorites (read: the romantic things). Here's my list.

1. scrapbook with me
2. compliment me on something that isn't physical
3. write me a note of five things you thought about me when we were first dating
4. tell me a way that knowing me has improved you as a person
5. plan a date night for us

And here are the ones I could do for you that would be outside my comfort zone.

1. initiate sex
2. use a sex toy
3. initiate a new sex act
4. shower with you
5. let you pick the TV show

I guess you sense a theme. And also, since I only watch TV a few minutes a night now, it would suck not to watch something I like. Anyway, I love you!

Love,

Elizabeth

12 How Do I Feel About Expressing Myself Verbally?

Many people, particularly women, bond through verbal expressions of love and long, deep conversations. However, this is not the love language of many men. When two partners with different bonding styles try to express love to one another, they can often end up feeling inadequate and frustrated. This e-mail will allow both partners to reflect on their thoughts about verbal communication and what it means to them to converse about deeper-level relationship issues.

Use the first prompt, as well as at least three others, and end with two or three open-ended questions!

- Writing this e-mail to you makes me feel _____.

- In my house, when I was growing up, emotions were expressed by _____.

- When I picture being close, this is the role of verbal emotional expression: _____.

- When I think of a fulfilling and meaningful conversation, these are a few topics that would be discussed: _____.

- When we currently talk, I do (or do not) feel close, because _____.

- When we try to have conversations, I feel that I am disappointing you, because _____.

- Ideally, here is how often I would want us to verbally communicate about topics that are meaningful to either of us: _____.

- Here is how I feel about small talk: _____.

- Here is how I feel about using e-mail to communicate about deeper issues, as we have been doing: _____.

Dear Kat,

I'm writing this to you with trepidation, because I know I have been a great source of disappointment to you in this area of our relationship. I know you think I'm hard to talk to and that I'm never serious, and I'm sorry.

In my house, my parents rarely talked about anything of consequence. Dad would drink, and Mom would obsessively cook and clean. Sometimes I heard them arguing behind closed doors, but aside from that, you wouldn't have known either of them had any emotions besides dissatisfaction. When I picture being close, verbal emotional expression doesn't play a big role. I picture us laughing together and hanging out, as well as being physically close. But talking about our feelings does not feel natural for me. That's why I tend to use humor and sarcasm. That's how Ron and I interacted growing up, and how we still do.

I'd like to talk on a deep level about once a week or so, but I can't see myself initiating it. I would like to hear how you're doing, and I can try to be open and receptive—and stop cracking jokes. I would like to hear some positives about your life, though. That is easier for me than just hearing the negatives, even though I know you're just venting. The e-mailing we've been doing is actually a good medium for us. It's easier for me to get into a serious frame of mind when I am writing.

Questions:

- Do you find me funny at all anymore? You barely crack a smile anymore, and you used to laugh all the time.
- Is a deep conversation once a week enough for you to feel good about us?

Yours, in all seriousness,
John

Dear John,

I feel wary about writing on this topic, because I am scared it will seem critical. I like to talk, and I like to talk about feelings. I know you tease me about this, but I don't generally like the teasing. It is important to me that we talk about things aside from what happened at work and what's for dinner—and that the conversations don't always turn into a comedy routine.

To me, verbal emotional expression is important. My parents didn't really talk to one another openly, but my mother confided in me a lot, probably more than was appropriate for my age at the time. But that's probably where I learned to value deep conversations. When you and I first met, we talked about how we grew up and about our hopes and goals for the future. I miss those types of conversations. Ideally, I would like us to sit down once a week without the kids and talk. When everything you say is a one-liner, I start to feel disconnected and lonely. That spills over into irritation and resentment.

I have noticed a difference in how I feel about you just since we started writing these e-mails. So I hope we keep this up after the book is done and after your "month trial" of this book is over.

Questions for you:

- Do you miss the conversations we used to have?

- Is this whole e-mail thing working for you?

- What topics do you wish we talked about more?

Love you,

Kat

How Do I Give and Receive Love?

13 Times I Felt Most Connected to You Recently

Although you and your partner may be feeling disconnected and detached—or even openly hostile—there are probably some recent times that you felt close. People often discount brief, everyday moments of connection. In this e-mail, you'll be focusing on these seconds or minutes during the day when you feel that you and your partner are on the same page.

Be specific when describing your connected moments. Don't just say, "I felt happy during our dinner out." Instead, say, "I felt close when you looked at me and told me you were glad to be there with me." Training yourself to focus on specific moments of intimate connection is healthy for your relationship, and you may realize that you and your partner still have a strong foundation.

Use the first prompt, as well as at least three others, and end with two or three open-ended questions!

- Writing this e-mail to you makes me feel _____.

- Here are three moments in the past month when I felt connected to you: _____.

- Here is why each of these as meaningful to me: _____.

- Each of these moments showcased the following positive qualities of yours: _____.

- I find it easy (or hard) to focus on small moments of connection, because _____.

- Growing up, I saw small moments of connection between my parents, like _____.

- Growing up, I did not see small moments of connection between my parents, instead, I saw _____.

- Here are some things you could do that would usually work to make me feel happier and closer: _____.

Dear Eric,

This is tough to write, since things have been so terrible lately. Still, I can think of two moments in the past month when I felt close to you. The first was when we went to the dog wash. I always like doing stuff with just you and Bobo, because when we first got together, it was always just us three. I felt close to you when I saw you talk to him before he got washed. The other time was when you put Emmy back to sleep after she'd had a nightmare.

Both moments showed me how warm and loving you can be. I would say that your being nice to the kids and the dog generally makes me feel warmer toward you. When I am angry with you, I find it hard to focus on small moments of connection, but I think it would be good if we could do it more.

- Do you have positive memories of me at all this month?

- Do you associate Bobo with us being in love?

Love,

Shannee

Dear Shannee,

I know you hate me right now because of all the money stuff, so we haven't had that many connected moments this month. It is hard for me to think of anything positive when I know you're so disappointed and angry. But here are a few.

- when you kissed me goodbye in the morning yesterday
- when you laughed at me playing horse with Emmy
- when you told me that Mark doesn't know Sophie's preschool teacher's name, which seemed to imply that I'm a better dad than he is

These made me feel connected, because I love any physical affection from you, and I love it when you seem happy or proud of me. You are a tough audience lately, though. I know this money thing was my fault, but I am not a bad guy overall.

Questions:

- Do you still love me at all?
- Were you serious when you were saying that it would be easier as a single mom?

I love you,

Eric

How Do I Give and Receive Love?

14 You Mean Well, But…

Now we will take a small detour from focusing on the positive. Instead, in this e-mail, you'll try to kindly and neutrally explain to your partner what she does that you really don't like, even if her actions are well intentioned. Some of these things you've likely shared with your partner already, and some may be new. The goal here is to save her from continuing to expend effort on things that don't make you happy— and to do this without embarrassing her. It can be hard to steer clear of sounding critical or harsh in this e-mail, so use this template to convey your sentiments in a productive way.

Dear _____,

When writing to you about things you do that I don't enjoy,
I feel _____. Here are three things that you tend to do
frequently that I don't enjoy, why I think you do them, how they
actually make me feel, and what we can try to do instead.

1. Behavior: _____

Why I think you do it: _____

How it makes me feel: _____

What we can do instead: _____

2. Behavior: _____

Why I think you do it: _____

How it makes me feel: _____

What we can do instead. _____

3. Behavior: _____

Why I think you do it: _____

How it makes me feel: _____

What we can do instead: _____

Make sure to end with two or three open-ended
questions!

Dear Elliot,

I feel really awkward writing this, because I don't want to hurt your feelings. Here are three things that you tend to do frequently that I don't enjoy, why I think you do them, how they actually make me feel, and what we can try to do instead.

1. Grabbing my boobs.

    I think you do this to be funny or to initiate sex.

    It makes me feel upset, like you don't care that I find this offensive and that it is physically painful.

    Instead, I would like a hug or a kiss.

2. Teasing me.

    I think you do this to be funny and because your family members tease each other.

    Teasing makes me feel embarrassed and annoyed.

    Instead, you could just be nice and gentle when we talk.

3. Public displays of affection.

    I think you do this because you love me and you enjoy it.

    It makes me feel awkward and embarrassed (except holding hands).

    Instead, we can hold hands, or you could put your arm around me.

Questions:

- Did this e-mail make you upset?
- Do you think these things would be hard for you to stop?

I love you,

Olivia

Dear Olivia,

I'm at a loss here, because there isn't much that you do with good intentions that I don't like, but I can come up with two for the sake of being agreeable. (You probably have ten for me.)

1. Cleaning the house together.

    You have said that you think this is fun, like we're a team.

    I think you do it because your parents used to do housework together.

    It makes me feel annoyed, because I don't have a lot of free time, and I don't want to spend it cleaning.

    Instead, I want you to let me hire a cleaning service.

2. Sending stuff to my mom.

    I think you do this to be nice both to me and to her.

    Since Mom doesn't reciprocate with gifts (to anyone), you end up upset, and then I get upset and frustrated.

    Instead, you could just give her one Christmas present and not expect anything back.

And the questions:

·   Can we hire a cleaning service?

·   Do you think Mom doesn't love you because she doesn't mention your gifts? Honestly, I think she doesn't know what to make of them—it's so different from how she is.

Love you,

Elliot

CHAPTER 4

Pursuers and Distancers

If you want to better understand your relationship with your partner, it is integral to recognize whether you're a pursuer or a distancer, a classic family-therapy concept introduced by Thomas Fogarty in 1979.[3] This dynamic occurs in greater or lesser intensity across the majority of relationships, and it can be observed even in the earliest days of courtship, if you look back closely. Sometimes, a person can be a pursuer in one relationship and a distancer in another, but you are likely consistent in your role within each relationship you're in.

When the couple is in a happy part of their relationship (such as the honeymoon stage), this pattern is less extreme. However, when a couple is under stress, this dynamic will become more obvious and may start to hurt the relationship. Although people cannot usually completely change their predisposition to these behaviors, they can learn to acknowledge and accept their own contribution to a pursuer-distancer dynamic, which allows them to interact in more moderate and adaptive ways.

Pursuers are romantic and love to feel known by and to truly know their partners. At the beginning of a relationship, the pursuer is often the one who envisions a future together. Pursuers are often passionate, lively, and dramatic. However, their desire to connect can be so great that it can sometimes feel suffocating. They want to talk all the time, schedule date nights, and be in contact throughout the day. When they feel ignored, abandoned, or betrayed, they can be mean and vindictive. They may accuse partners of lying and cheating and may say cruel things in the heat of anger. Pursuers can become frantic when they fear that a partner doesn't understand them, and they often feel lonely in a marriage that seems perfectly fine to their partners.

Distancers are typically calm, cool, and collected. They usually don't want to talk when they are at work or with friends, and they want to make plans with others or on their own instead of prioritizing couple time. They enjoy groups more than one-on-one time, because conversation stays more light. At first, distancers seem steady and laid back, but over time, they can start to seem cold and arrogant.

Distancers don't often enjoy talking deeply about relationships, except a bit during the honeymoon stage. They withdraw during arguments, and—very strangely, from the perspective of a pursuer—they can easily go to sleep after, or in the middle of, an argument. Distancers avoid confrontation. They say things like "I'm not mad" when they really are, which is frustrating to their pursuer partners. Frequently, distancers avoid expressing their opinions, but they then may explode over an issue and dredge up unspoken complaints from years earlier. They can also be passive-aggressive and communicate their anger with indirect insults, nonverbal communication like eye rolling, or failing to do something they promised to do.

❤15 Pursuer or Distancer?

Even if you're not as extreme as these descriptions of pursuers and distancers, you still likely fall more toward one category. Sometimes, people are pursuers in one relationship but distancers in others. However, in your main intimate relationship (such as your marriage), you tend toward your natural role, the one that you subconsciously learned in childhood. Here's a hint: if you're the one who purchased this book, you're likely the pursuer. And if you're the one who said, "Nah, we don't really need this book" or have avoided doing the exercises, you're the distancer.

If you find yourself thinking that your partner is an extreme pursuer or distancer, but you're not as extreme, look more carefully at yourself. It is highly unlikely to be the case. Extreme pursuers and distancers tend to find one another, and neither generally feels a spark with people who are in the middle of the spectrum. Also, two pursuers or two distancers don't usually click; they seek their opposite.

Use the first prompt, as well as at least three others, and end with two or three open-ended questions!

- Writing you this e-mail makes me feel _____.

- I think I am the pursuer (or distancer) in this relationship, because _____.

- One example of when we most recently fell into this pattern is _____.

- Here is how I feel about being in this dynamic with you: _____.

- When you pursue (or distance yourself), it makes me feel _____.

Dear Dave,

I feel excited to write you this e-mail, because, hello, this is us. I am, of course, the pursuer, and you are the distancer. I always text you, want to make plans in advance, and try to get you to open up. And you're always evading me! We fell into this pattern just this morning, when I was asking when you'll be home tonight, and you kept saying you didn't know and that you can't focus at work if you have to report to me what time you'll be home. But I could have picked any of a dozen other examples.

Pursuing is not fun for me. But when you distance yourself, I get anxious and scared that you're not committed to me and that you're going to leave me, like you did with Dara.

My questions:

- Did you immediately recognize us in this pattern too?

- Did Dara also act like a pursuer with you?

I love you, baby,

Farrah

Dear Farrah,

I feel hesitant writing this e-mail to you. I know what you're going to say—that I'm the distancer here. I agree that some of the description fits, but not everything. I am fine with spending a lot of time with you. I love you. The problem is when you tell me that I can't do anything without checking in. Then it's like you're my mom, not my wife. I don't want to feel like I have to keep you at a distance, but if I don't set boundaries, I fear that I'll end up having no independent thoughts or life at all. When you pursue me, I feel suffocated and resentful.

The most recent example of us doing this was when I told you about John's bachelor party, and you flipped out. I should have given you more notice, but you acted like it was this big example of how I don't think about you. To me, though, it's just a party. When you get mad like that, I shut down, because it seems like talking will just make things worse.

- Do you think that if you laid off me a little, we would be able to get along better?
- Do you think I am "cold and arrogant"?

Love,

Dave

16 Childhood Origins of This Pattern

Pursuers and distancers are created in childhood. If a parent is unpredictable—sometimes distant and unapproachable, but sometimes fun and affectionate—a child will usually devote considerable effort to getting this parent's attention, hoping for the parent's loving side to come out. This child will likely turn into a pursuer in adult relationships. Children who witness volatile, dramatic relationships also often become pursuers, since they yearn for the perfect relationship that they never saw at home.

Distancers are usually created in one of two types of families. The first type is the unemotional family, in which independence is prioritized over closeness. These kids' parents told them to go play and not to cry, and the parents didn't engage in open displays of affection or conversations about feelings. Over time, distancers learned that just not having any feelings is easier than having feelings that are not recognized or understood. Distancers can also come from chaotic and conflicted families, in which emotional expression always ended badly, or they may have had intrusive parents who gave them no space to have private feelings. Either way, distancers generally believe that emotions are bad, dangerous, and childish, and they do their best never to feel any.

Use the first prompt, as well as at least three others, and end with two or three open-ended questions!

- Writing this e-mail to you makes me feel _____.

- Here is how I would describe my relationship with each of my parents: _____.

- This is the type of relationship that I witnessed between my parents: _____.

- I think I pursue (or distance myself) because I got used to doing it from my parent (or parents) in this way: _____.

- Here is what I learned about expressing emotions from growing up in my family: _____.

- Here is what I learned about independence (or relying on others) from growing up in my family: _____.

Make sure to end with two or three open-ended questions!

Dear Vincent,

I feel awkward writing this e-mail to you, because it brings up stuff that I don't really think about. My parents' relationship could best be described as "strained" or "tense." My mom was always upset about how much Dad worked. Then, when she died, my dad almost forgot that he even had kids. My aunts and uncles stepped in and took care of us, while dad drank and became even more distant.

Mom was great, and it was hard for me when she passed. I tried to get my dad to hang out with me, but it never worked. I also think he already suspected I was gay, and he kept his distance even more because of that.

I think I distance myself from you because I learned so early that it is better to be self-reliant than to depend on anyone for anything. I didn't realize I was that way until you brought it up, but I see now why it makes sense.

- What did you learn about relationships from seeing your parents?

- Does this help you understand more about why I am a "closed book," as you say?

Your "distancer,"

Henry

Dear Henry,

I'm looking forward to writing you this e-mail, because it is stuff I've been talking about in therapy. I've begun to realize over the past year that my relationship with my mom was pretty messed up. I knew she was difficult, but my therapist thinks she may have had borderline personality disorder. She was moody and unpredictable, flew into rages, and thought everyone was always talking about her. But, people with borderline personality disorder are also really charming at times, and they can make others really love them.

That's the thing about Mom—when she was "on," she was awesome. I always kept hanging around her, even when she was mean, because I hoped she would turn back into her loving and fun self. Her mood set the tone of the house, and I focused on how to make her happy. I learned that emotions are intense and scary, and you can't count on anyone feeling the same about you from one minute to the next.

I think my relationship with Mom led me to act the same way with you, which explains why I'm always hanging around, calling too much, making plans too far in advance—all the things that bother you. I am just insecure about anyone loving me consistently, so I try to get them to commit more and more. You are hard to pin down, and this makes me more anxious, and I act even clingier.

Questions:

- What do you remember from your mom and dad's marriage before she passed away?

- What was your dad like with his second wife?

- What did you learn about emotions at home?

> I love you, honey,
>
> Vincent

17 How My Pursuing (or Distancing) Hurts Us

Pursuers and distancers pair off with each other and then exacerbate each other's issues. Distancers can make pursuers feel insecure and unloved, and pursuers can make distancers feel smothered and controlled. Extreme distancers often want a friends-with-benefits type of relationship, even in their marriages. No lovey-dovey stuff, just companionship and sex, with both partners frequently engaging in activities outside the relationship. Distancers prize independence over interdependence, which can make their partners feel lonely and disconnected.

Pursuers, on the other hand, long for a romantic, soulmate connection. They ask for interdependence, but this often manifests as codependence. Pursuers have extremely high standards for relationships, and when they feel that an idealized connection is not within reach, they become extremely upset. Over time, they may even disconnect from the relationship out of hopelessness.

Becoming aware of your role in the pursuer-distancer pattern can help you and your partner modify your dynamic so it feels more comfortable and secure for both.

Distancers often engage in behaviors such as

- not picking up their phones;

- prioritizing hobbies and friends over the relationship;

- minimizing or denying their own emotions ("I'm not mad");

- refusing to schedule date nights;

- refusing to consider couples therapy;

- ignoring a partner's distress (such as not comforting a crying partner); and

- dismissing a partner's feelings.

Pursuers often engage in behaviors such as

- texting or calling excessively;

- trying to pin down their partners for plans far in advance;

- being jealous of a partner's friendships or hobbies;

- turning down sex to punish a partner for emotional distance;

- flirting with other people or threatening to cheat, when feeling upset about the relationship; and

- saying cruel things in anger.

Choose a few of the above behaviors—or others that you can think of—and describe (1) why you do them, (2) how you feel about doing them, and (3) their impact on your partner and relationship. Be sure to end with two or three open-ended questions!

Dear Rob,

I am the distancer here, so...

- I don't pick up my phone when you call because I'm busy at work and conversations with you can last a long time. I sometimes feel guilty when I don't pick up, but other times I just feel relieved. I think not picking up the phone can actually be positive for our relationship sometimes, because then you find something to do besides talk to me, but I know it hurts your feelings to know that I'm screening your calls.

- I minimize my emotions—and yours too—because you get really angry, and I don't know how to deal with it. Sometimes I'm angry, but I don't want to say anything, because if I do, you say whatever you're feeling is worse. I know that denying feelings is bad for the relationship, but I don't know what else to do.

- I don't refuse to consider couples therapy, but I don't have the time right now. If we are still struggling this summer, I will do it.

Questions:

- What else can I do to make things better when you are so mad at me?

- Do you have a couples counselor in mind? You mentioned your own therapist, but I don't know if I like that idea.

Love,

Stacey

Dear Stacey,

Here are the behaviors I do. I'll stick to three, but we know there are more.

- I say mean things when I am angry. I am trying to work on this. I do it because I am so mad that I literally see red. My dad did it too, and that makes me feel even worse. It hurts you and our relationship.

- I am jealous of how much time you spend with your coworkers. Maybe if you invited me more, it would help. I know my jealousy makes things worse, but I don't know how to accept that in addition to a fifty-hour workweek, you want to hang out with your coworkers at happy hour all the time.

- I threaten to end our relationship when I am angry. I don't really want to end things, but sometimes I don't think you love me. I am trying to work on this in therapy, realizing that you may love me but don't express it the way I expect.

Questions:

- Do you see any changes in me since I started therapy? If so, what are they?

- Why don't you want me at happy hour with your work friends?

Love,

Rob

18 How Can We Stop Pursuing and Distancing?

In order to extricate themselves from an extremely toxic pursuer-distancer dynamic, both partners need to recognize their individual contributions to the pattern. Then they can think of alternative behaviors to create a healthier dynamic. For example, if a distancing husband made a point to set aside time each week for a date night with his pursuing wife, she may, in turn, feel less like she has to pursue him for attention. Similarly, if a pursuing wife decided to go back to school and focus on her own goals, this might help her to stop obsessing about the relationship, which would stop her distancer husband feeling that he has to be there for her constantly.

Use the first prompt, as well as at least three others, and end with two or three open-ended questions!

- Writing you this e-mail makes me feel _____.

- Here are three ways that I could try to stop pursuing (or distancing): _____.

- Here are three ways that you could make me feel more secure, which would help me change my pursuing (or distancing) behavior: _____.

- Here is what we could say to each other if we notice that we are falling into the pursuer-distancer pattern: _____.

- Here are situations that exacerbate our pattern, which we could try to watch out for or avoid: _____.

- Here is one time when we were in the pursuer-distancer pattern recently, and how we could have handled it differently: _____.

Dear Sarah,

I feel embarrassed writing you this e-mail, because I am ashamed of my most recent pursuing behavior (Saturday, when I kept texting you when you were out). Three ways that I could try to stop pursuing: reminding myself that you love me, not drinking as much, and starting therapy again. Three ways that you could help me stop: being more emotionally present when we're together (not on our phones), planning date nights, and giving me a set time when you'll be home. It's difficult for me when I feel uncertain about how much you really care about me, so if you try to show me that you love me more openly and frequently—and don't say I am "needy" or "clingy," it would be easier for me to stop obsessing over where you are and when you'll be back.

Questions:

- What do you tell your friends about our relationship?
- Do you ever get jealous?

Love,

Annemarie

Dear Annemarie,

I feel upset writing this e-mail to you, because I feel that your behavior on Saturday was out of line and seriously made me question everything. If you didn't drink when I went out, I am sure you would be able to control yourself and not get so angry. But there is also a greater jealousy and depression issue.

My part in all of this is that I allow you to sweep your drinking (and depression) under the rug, as part of my distancing, I guess. I think you should try AA again. At the very least, you need to resume with your therapist. I have not been as supportive as I should be about your drinking or your depression, and I can do better. My tendency is to withdraw when things are hard, and I know that makes everything worse for you, so I am sorry. I will try to be more loving and comforting to you, but on your end, I would like you to commit to making your mental and physical health a priority again.

Questions:

- How many months did you not drink that time you quit before you met me?

- Are you willing to try antidepressants?

I love you,
Sarah

19 Our Pursuer-Distancer Dynamic in Bed

Ironically, the one place that pursuers and distancers will often exchange roles is in the bedroom. The distancer often wants more sex, but the pursuer doesn't want sex, because of the perceived absence of emotional closeness. This contributes to this couple's vicious cycle, because, often, distancers let their guard down only during sex and will open up emotionally only when they feel physically intimate.

Sometimes, a couple actually enjoys the pursuer-distancer dynamic in bed, because the pursuer enjoys the thrill of the chase, and the distancer enjoys being chased. However, it is likely that at least one partner would like the pattern to change in some of the encounters. This e-mail can also be viewed as a practice e-mail for chapter 8, where you will be discussing your sexual relationship.

Use the first prompt, as well as at least three others, and end with two to three open-ended questions!

- Writing to you about this topic makes me feel _____.

- I am the pursuer (or distancer) in bed, and this makes me feel _____.

- I like (or do not like) our sexual dynamic, because _____.

- Our sexual dynamic has changed from our earlier relationship in this way: _____.

- Sometimes I find myself pursuing (or distancing myself) in bed, because of other issues in our relationship, like _____.

- Changing this dynamic when we are intimate would make me feel _____.

Dear Lila,

I feel resentful writing to you about this topic, because it's been a point of contention. I am obviously the pursuer in bed, and this makes me feel rejected, like you don't love me. I am not only the pursuer, I am also the only one who even seems to enjoy sex. I hate this dynamic, because I feel lonely and unloved. I miss how we used to be, when you seemed to actually like touching me.

Sometimes I feel myself pursuing you in bed just to see if you'll respond. I want sex, but more than that, I want you to pay attention to me, rather than looking through me. If we changed our dynamic in bed, it would make me feel worlds better. It is terrible to feel like your own wife can't stand the sight of you.

Questions:

- Were you faking it in the first years of our relationship, or were you really into it then?

- Is there anything I could do to excite you anymore?

- Is there any connection between how much stuff I do around the house and how much you want sex? Sometimes it seems like an inverse correlation!

Love,

Eddie

Dear Eddie,

This e-mail is hard for me to write, since I know you're really angry about this topic. I'm the distancer in bed, which I feel is so strange, because otherwise I am pursuing you all the time, pushing you to commit to time together, to do stuff around the house, and to be involved as a husband and father. But, in bed, I certainly distance myself from you. I hate the dynamic, but I know how it evolved.

At the beginning of our relationship, I thought you were committed to me, and I felt secure and happy. Over time, you pulled away and focused mainly on work. You're way less involved with me emotionally than you were when I was into sex, and this is no coincidence. I can't be physically intimate with a man who I think sees me as the nanny and the cook.

I would love to be more physically intimate, but we need to work on everything else in our relationship first.

Questions:

- When you ask for sex, do you think about the status of our relationship otherwise? Like, if we are fighting, does it ever occur to you *not* to ask?

- Is sex separate from love for you?

- Do you miss how we used to be emotionally, or do you just miss the sex?

XX,

Lila

CHAPTER 5

Trust

Many people wonder whether they can really trust their partner to be there for them, on an everyday basis as well as in a crisis. This feeling of uncertainty is compounded dramatically if there has been a history of infidelity or dishonesty. It is essential that you trust that your partner will show you affection on a regular basis, will listen to your problems and celebrate your victories with you, and will not dismiss or invalidate your feelings. That is why we discuss the roles of empathy and validation in promoting trust in a relationship.

20 Empathy

Empathy is the ability to truly see another person's perspective. You don't have to feel the same way, but you have to understand why the other person feels this way, given his unique circumstances, history, and background. You can empathize with anyone, even serial killers. Given their probably traumatic childhood and sociopathic traits, it does make sense that they might go down the path they did. Now, if you can empathize with a serial killer, empathizing with your partner should (hopefully!) be easy.

Use the first prompt, as well as at least three others, and end with two or three open-ended questions!

- Writing to you about empathy makes me feel _____.

- I think I am good (or bad) at empathy, because _____.

- I think that I am most empathic to you about _____.

- You are most empathic to me about _____.

- I think I need to work on being more empathic to you about _____.

- In my house growing up, the person who was empathic to me was _____.

- I did (or did not) witness empathy between my parents, and this impacted me by _____.

- I would like you to express your empathy in this way: _____.

Dear Eve,

I feel fine writing to you about empathy. It's not something I am naturally good at, since my house was more of a survival-of-the-fittest environment. The only person who was empathic was my grandma, but she wasn't around a lot. I need to work on empathizing with you more about your migraines and your stomach issues. I never get sick, so I can't understand what it's like. You, on the other hand, are always empathic to me and the kids, and to your students too. That's why you're so great at what you do, and why I work in an office with other robots like myself—ha.

My questions:

- Who was the most empathic person in your house growing up?
- Do you think I am better with sympathizing about your migraines and IBS than I was earlier in our marriage?

Yours,

Cody

Dear Cody,

I feel upset writing about this to you, because you really hurt my feelings the other day when you accepted the BBQ invite with the "joke" about me probably not being able to come. I have never missed a day of work due to migraines or IBS, which my friends and doctors say is amazing, but that means I am wiped out during the weekend, so sometimes I have to miss social obligations even though I wish I didn't. I think you definitely should work on your empathy, and you probably are the way you are because your dad is so unempathic. My mom was always kind and understanding about my physical and emotional problems, so I learned to be that way from her.

You are good with empathizing about my work stress, but as soon as it crosses into the physical realm, I feel like you dismiss me. I would appreciate if you would tell me that you understand that my pain is real, and if you would say, "I feel so bad you're in pain, tell me what I could do to help."

My questions:

- Do you really think I am faking when I get a migraine or a flare-up?

- Do you think you're dismissive about my migraines because your mom has them and your dad is always acting like she's just being a princess?

Thank you for reading this,

Eve

21 Validation and Invalidation

One great way to express empathy is using validation. When you validate your partner, you're saying that his perspective makes sense to you. Even if you disagree with him, you can still validate him, saying something like, "That makes sense, given your feelings about the situation or your background or your experience."

The opposite of validation is invalidation. This is when you tell someone that her feelings are "wrong" or "silly," or that she is not thinking or feeling the way she "should" be. Dismissing, minimizing, shaming, or gaslighting (convincing someone that she is crazy) are all forms of invalidation, as are nonverbal responses like eye rolling or sighing.

Chronic invalidation can poison relationships, making it impossible for partners to feel safe expressing their feelings. If you grew up in an invalidating home, you were likely told, "That's nothing to be upset about," "You're being ridiculous," "That's silly," and "You're crying over nothing." As an adult with a history of being invalidated, it is likely that your automatic default is to invalidate your partner's feelings, particularly if you feel attacked.

In this e-mail, we'll discuss validation in your relationship, and how to change your relationship to be more accepting and less dismissing.

Use the first prompt, as well as at least three others, and end with two or three open-ended questions!

- Writing about validation and invalidation makes me feel _____.

- Here's an example of one time that you validated (or invalidated) me recently, and how this made me feel: _____.

- My mother (or father) was validating (or invalidating) in these ways: _____.

- Here's one time I validated (or invalidated) you recently: _____.

- I will commit to trying to validate you more, especially about _____.

Dear Lisa,

I feel strange writing this e-mail to you, because I've never heard of invalidation before literally right now, but I will give this a shot. One time you validated me recently was when I explained how John was being a real jerk at work, and you agreed that he has really been riding me lately. That made me feel good—that you noticed how he's changed. One time you invalidated me was when I wanted to watch the game, and you said it's ridiculous that I want to sit on the couch on such a nice day. That made me feel angry; I work all week, and I should be able to choose what I want to do without you giving me an attitude.

My mother was pretty invalidating, I guess, because she was always telling me how silly I was, and she never believed me when I told her how Seth would beat me up and take my stuff. My dad was neutral; he would never say that my opinions made sense, but he also didn't say I was being stupid.

I invalidated you the other day when I told you that sitting around scrapbooking is much more of a waste of a nice day than watching football, and I'm sorry. I will commit to trying to validate you more about your intelligence and how great a wife you are.

Questions:

- Can you think of other times when I was invalidating?
- Do you think I am usually invalidating?

Love,

Kyle

Dear Kyle,

I am excited to write this e-mail to you, since it gives a word to what I have been trying to tell you for years. When you roll your eyes and act like I'm being annoying and childish, that is really invalidating, and it makes me really angry. I probably react this way because my mom also acts like that, and when I was little, she would always tell me, "You don't know how lucky you are," just because I didn't grow up with an alcoholic dad like hers. But she didn't consider how bad it was to have a mom who always seemed disappointed in me.

You were validating recently when you admitted that I did gain weight since the wedding. I know that seems weird, but it is so awkward when I complain, and then you pretend that it's all in my head. I also liked that you said it doesn't matter to you.

On the other side, you were invalidating when you told me that my mom has a point about not going into nursing. I think nursing would be a great career for when we have kids, and so what if she didn't like it. She's not me.

I tried to validate you recently—when I told you that I agree that you're getting a lot of flak from John lately—but I was invalidating last night, when I told you that sex shouldn't be so important to you. I was lying anyway. I think sex is important too.

Questions:

- Was your dad validating when you were a kid?

- Did you recognize that invalidation is the thing that I always say that you do to me?

XOXO,

Lisa

Trust

22 Empathic Ruptures

Empathic ruptures are times when one partner feels that the other showed a marked lack of empathy and understanding during a particularly vulnerable moment. On my website, http://www.drpsychmom.com, a reader discussed losing weight and getting up the nerve to schedule a photo shoot of sexy Valentine's Day pictures for her husband. His reaction was silence, and she felt devastated. This is a sad example of an empathic rupture; one partner expects or needs a loving and supportive response, and the other does not provide it. Sometimes this partner doesn't know how to respond, sometimes he doesn't even understand that there is a response required, and sometimes he feels angry and consciously withholds a supportive response. No matter what the reason, empathic ruptures can lead to deep-seated resentment and bitterness, almost akin to the betrayal felt when a partner is unfaithful.

This e-mail may be painful to write, but it has the potential to be healing. Your goal is to explain, in a nonconfrontational way, why you felt so hurt by your partner's behavior during a particular incident. You will also discuss why you were so triggered by this rupture, based on your past experiences.

Use the first prompt, as well as at least three others, and end with two or three open-ended questions!

- Writing this e-mail to you makes me feel _____.

- The empathic rupture that I most want to discuss is _____.

- When it happened, I felt _____.

- When we have discussed it since then, I have felt _____.

- If I try hard to think about why this episode was so upsetting to me, I realize that it is because _____.

- Something I never told you about this empathic rupture is _____.

- I was particularly triggered by this because, in my childhood, similar things happened: _____.

- I would feel better about this incident if you _____.

- In the future, if something like this happens, I will commit to (or I hope you commit to) _____.

Dear Jane,

I feel apprehensive writing this e-mail to you, because I don't like to dredge up old issues, but our worst empathic rupture was when you told Josh that we were fighting. To me, that was a betrayal. He never got over you, and if I didn't see the texts and shut it all down, I know he would have told you to leave me. I never told you this, but when I first met you, I was intimidated by Josh. He was everything I was not, and your parents loved him. So when you confided in him about us, it was a slap in the face.

When I was a kid, Mom would always talk about me to her family. She would tell them I was "a bad seed." In retrospect, I think it was just a joke, but it hurt. Until they figured out that I had ADHD, everyone thought I was just bad. When you talked about me to Josh, I was triggered, because it was another person I loved telling someone about how bad I am.

In the future, I would like you never to tell him anything personal about us. I will try to be more open and not so loud and angry, which I know makes you upset. I love you, and I think we are past this, but then again, I still think about it.

My questions:

- Do you understand why this was so difficult for me?
- Are you honest about not telling him stuff like that anymore?
- Are you aware that he is in love with you?

Love,

Will

Dear Will,

I am terrified writing you this e-mail, because I don't want us to take a step backward. But I think it's essential to talk about everything openly instead of you raging at me and me running to my friends and family for support. That's why I like these e-mails, because it doesn't get nasty between us.

Our worst empathic rupture for me was the time that you called me "a slob" in front of my mom. You know how I am always trying to clean up when she comes over, because she can be really critical. I know you say you were joking, but it wasn't funny. Also, you saw how upset I was, and you didn't come after me when I walked out.

When I was a kid, my dad called me "Pigpen"—after the character from the Charlie Brown cartoon—and I would laugh, but I was hurt. I am sensitive about my mom judging me and also about being perceived as a mess, so your remark was the worst of both worlds. I would feel better about this incident if you genuinely apologized and didn't add "but it was a joke" or "but you overreacted."

Questions:

- How did you feel when you saw how upset I was after you said that?

- Do you think it's stupid that this is what I chose for this e-mail and that it's from two years ago?

Love,

Jane

23 What Commitment Means to Me

If either partner in a long-term relationship feels that the other is looking for a way out or would leave if a better opportunity presented itself, this will lead to guardedness, distance, and dissatisfaction. If you've discussed ending the relationship, this is a time to clarify your commitment level. For example, you can commit to remaining together with no talk of ending the relationship for at least six months, including time spent writing the e-mails in this book and refocusing on your relationship. Alternately, you can lay out your boundaries, telling your partner which circumstances would lead to you leaving. And of course, if you are feeling positive about the future, this is an ideal time to reassure your partner of your commitment.

Use the first prompt, as well as at least three others, and end with two or three open-ended questions!

- Writing about this topic to you makes me feel _____.

- When I think of the word *commitment*, I feel _____.

- When I was younger, I felt that commitment meant _____.

- From my parents, I learned that commitment was _____.

- Now, I feel commitment means _____.

- I am committed to our relationship, because _____.

- When I think of losing you, I feel _____.

- I know that you are committed to this relationship, because _____.

- I think (or do not think) about ending this relationship, because _____.

- I have (or have not ever) thought about ending our relationship, because _____.

- I would seriously consider ending this relationship if _____.

- I want to take a break and reevaluate our relationship, because _____.

- I want to get back together, because _____.

- I will know that I am ready to commit to you permanently when _____.

Dear Anthony,

I feel awkward writing this to you, because we haven't fully discussed what I want to do moving forward. I am feeling better, particularly since you've been opening up, but that in no way means that I have forgiven you for cheating. I want us to remain in separate apartments for now, but we can continue to see each other and e-mail like we have been doing.

To me, commitment means the desire to be together, forever, no matter what. I never seriously considered even flirting with another guy while we were together, so what you did was alien to me, as well as devastating and traumatic. I know that, to you, kissing someone else was not designed to hurt me, and I think that you are changing how you view flirtations. But to me, commitment is all or nothing. Even my parents, who fought all the time, never cheated on each other. Yes, kissing is cheating and so is flirting. If we do get back together, I want you to know that any flirting would cause me to leave immediately.

Questions:

- What does commitment mean to you?

- Do you think the fact that your dad cheated on your mom impacts how you viewed kissing that girl?

- Do you fully understand how humiliated I felt?

Thank you for reading,

Sarah

Dear Sarah,

I feel upset writing this to you. I know that I made you feel terrible. I hope you let me come back home soon, because I miss you so much. To me, commitment means that you take care of your partner through thick and thin and that you never let them down. I know that I let you down doing what I did, but please know that even if you dumped me, I would still always be there for you if you ever needed me. Before this happened, I thought that flirting was okay, although I now know that it was wrong. I never wanted to leave you. I want to be with you forever. I know I was wrong. For what it's worth, if you kissed someone, I would be mad, but I wouldn't end things. However, if you slept with someone, I would (and I never would have done that).

Questions:

- Does it matter to you that it didn't mean anything when I kissed her?
- Are you going to let me come back home?

Love,

Anthony

24 Infidelity

Discovering that a partner has been unfaithful can be a cataclysmic blow to a relationship. Everyone has a different definition for infidelity. For some couples, infidelity is texting flirtatiously, and for others, it is having an ongoing affair with both sexual and emotional intimacy. No matter its definition, partners tend to respond to infidelity in certain ways. There is initial shock, hurt, and anger, followed by the desire to know every detail about the betrayal, and then, hopefully, a period during which the unfaithful partner can empathize with and apologize to the betrayed partner, who can choose whether or not to forgive and move forward in the relationship.

In a best-case scenario, couples who decide to remain together can use the infidelity as a springboard for creating a new and closer relationship. This can happen only if both partners are open to understanding the other's experiences, including thoughts and feelings about the relationship, about the affair, and about the future of the relationship. If the betrayed partner understands why her partner cheated, this may allow her to empathize and, eventually, to forgive. If forgiveness is not possible, then understanding and acceptance can sometimes be enough to allow a couple to move forward.

It is helpful to discuss whether anything in the relationship made one or both partners decide to look for emotional or physical intimacy elsewhere. But this isn't always the case, as many people who are satisfied with their relationship also cheat, out of a desire to explore something new, a need to bolster their self-esteem, or a tendency toward impulsive or self-sabotaging behavior.

In this e-mail, you and your partner can continue any discussion you have had about past infidelities within a framework that can prevent explosive and unproductive fights. Couples who haven't experienced infidelity can choose the prompts that help them discuss other facets of this topic.

Use the first prompt, as well as at least three others, and end with two or three open-ended questions!

- Writing about infidelity to you makes me feel _____.

- When you (or I) discovered the infidelity, I felt _____.

- If I try to be objective, I believe that the infidelity occurred because _____.

- In my childhood (or adolescence), here is what I thought (or observed) about infidelity: _____.

- In my past relationships, infidelity occurred when _____.

- The idea of you being unfaithful makes me feel _____.

- I consider infidelity to be _____.

- In order for us to repair our relationship, these things need to happen: _____.

- When I think about my (or your) infidelity, I feel _____.

- From the infidelity, I have learned _____.

- I hope that discussing the infidelity can allow us to move forward and grow in these ways _____.

- I am sorry about _____.

Dear Iris,

I feel ashamed writing about this to you. I think we are over the worst of everything now, but you still bring it up all the time, so we'll probably never be over it. Anyway, when you discovered that I was seeing Cara, I felt terrified. As I've told you, it wasn't anything serious. If I think about it objectively, I think it was because she came on to me, and I was a drunk idiot. It continued because you and I were fighting, and I convinced myself that you wouldn't even care, since you didn't want to sleep with me yourself.

I feel terrible, and I want to rebuild things. As you know, my dad cheated, and I never wanted to be like him. I always thought he was a real loser for hurting my mom. But now I understand how it might have happened, although that doesn't make it right for him or for me.

To fix things, I will show you that I will never be unfaithful again. I will go to counseling, if you want, although I really don't think we need to rehash everything with a third party. I love you, and I am sorry. Let's try and move forward, for the kids and for us.

Questions:

- How long do you think it will take until you trust me again?
- What did you tell your family?

Love,

Harry

Dear Harry,

I feel nauseous writing this e-mail to you, but that's how I always feel nowadays. When I found out, it was like I'd been hit by a truck. I wanted to kill you. I kept remembering what you told me about your dad cheating on your mom, and I thought you were a huge phony.

I do not know if we will fully recover as a couple, and it will be almost impossible for me to ever trust you again. If you want to make things easier, you could give me all your passwords and have yourself transferred to a different division, where you have no chance of seeing her. Maybe that would show me that you're really committed to staying married, that you're not feeding me a line.

If I am objective, I think you cheated because we were fighting, and you needed an ego boost. I also think that you learned from your dad that lying and cheating are okay.

Questions:

- Will you give me your passwords and switch divisions?
- Will you leave this job if they don't let you switch divisions?

Your wife,

Iris

25 Repairing Trust in Everyday Ways

In this e-mail, you will have the opportunity to ask your partner to behave in ways that may help you trust her on a deeper level. Note that the first ten suggested activities are more relevant to pursuers, and the second ten are more relevant to distancers (see chapter 4 for more on pursuers and distancers). While these activities may not all seem to be directly related to improving trust, they all promote feeling emotionally secure and safe, which is a prerequisite for trust. The last five activities are about trusting that a partner will be faithful and is content within a monogamous relationship. These will likely be most relevant to those who have experienced or who fear infidelity.

You will ask your partner via e-mail to do two or three of these activities in the coming week, and hopefully, you will also commit to trying the activities that your partner requests. In the response e-mail, you and your partner should confirm your commitment to trying the suggested behaviors during the coming week. If your partner agrees to try them, express appreciation and gratitude, and, if not, perhaps she will be ready to try later in the process. You can print this list at http://www.newharbinger/34602.com so you can look at it in coming weeks and discuss with your partner the possibility of doing more of these activities to further increase trust and security.

- Pick up your phone if I call this week, and if you can't, text me back within the hour.

- Sit down with me twice this week just to talk.

- Plan a date night for us this week.

- Tell me you love me every day this week.

- Kiss me when you come home each day this week.

- Have a conversation with me about whether we should start couples counseling.

- If you see that I am upset, ask me what's wrong and give me a hug.

- Try not to invalidate me or tell me that my feelings are wrong or overreactions.

- Don't look at your phone when we talk.

- Don't do any work from home at least one evening this week.

- Don't ask me where I've been if I don't pick up my phone.

- Don't imply that I am unfaithful or flirting with other people.

- Don't look through my phone.

- Sit down with the calendar and tell me which nights are best for me to see my friends.

- Give me a half hour when I come home from work before you initiate a discussion.

- Don't text repeatedly if I don't respond immediately.

- Don't scream or cry if I do something you don't like; try to calmly tell me what is wrong.

- Don't threaten to end the relationship.

- Don't say negative things about me or my family.

- Don't bring up emotional topics when I am leaving for work.

- In front of others or to me, say positive things about being in a committed relationship with me.

- Mention that you have a partner in casual conversation with someone who is attractive.

- Talk positively about me to your friends.

- When someone flirts with you, tell me about it right away.

- When you interact with an ex, tell me about it right away.

Use all of these prompts to write your e-mail, and don't forget to add two or three of the activities above!

- Writing this e-mail makes me feel _____.

- If you do these three activities, I will feel _____.

- I know these will be hard for you, because _____.

- I can make these things easier for you by _____.

Dear Evan,

I feel worried about writing this, because I don't want you to take it badly. My suggestions are: don't call me at work this week, don't ask whether I've had contact with James, and don't bring up anything important in the mornings before work. I would feel happy and relieved if you did those for a week. I know they would be hard for you, and again, I am really sorry that I did anything to damage your trust. I love you, but I can't feel like I'm on trial anymore.

I can make these things easier by calling you from work if I have a minute, telling you more about my day when I get home, and sitting down to talk in the evenings instead of doing work.

I love you,

Nora

Dear Nora,

I feel resentful writing you this e-mail, because I doubt you're going to do the things I ask. I hate being in this place, and as you know, I still think about what happened between you and James every day, but let's not go down that road. My requests:

- Openly tell me each day if James has contacted you, so I don't have to harass you about it.

- Don't bring work home at least for a couple of nights this week.

- Mention that you're happy in our relationship in front of other people.

I would feel relieved if you would do these three things. I would feel like you understand how badly you hurt me. I know they would be hard for you, because work is your life, and because you never like to bring up topics that lead to conflict. But I could make them easier on you by trying to not mention him unless you tell me that he contacted you, and we talk about it then. Also, I'll try to complain less when I see you on the computer.

Thanks for considering this,

Evan

Trust

CHAPTER 6

Apologies

After the previous chapter's work, we will turn to apologizing for empathic ruptures, misunderstandings, lies, and infidelities. Even if partners have apologized in the past, a carefully written e-mail is an excellent way to clarify all of your thoughts and feelings. Your partner will then have a full and genuine apology to read and reread when he feels sad or insecure. Even if your partner does not forgive you for a given behavior or event, your expressions of regret and sorrow may allow him to feel that the relationship is moving forward in healthy ways.

Keep in mind that many people did not grow up hearing their parents apologize. In many families, problems were swept under the rug, or they led to explosions and were never brought up again. If this resonates with you, you likely haven't had much practice in the art of apologizing. These e-mails will help you give the gift of an authentic and meaningful apology to your partner. For many couples, this will allow long standing hurts to be validated, paving the way for reparations.

26 Ways That You Have Hurt Me

In this e-mail, you will focus on three ways that your partner has hurt you. Even if you have told your partner how he has hurt you hundreds of times, it is likely that you have not used the most healthy communication strategies to do so. Anger and frustration can get in the way of expressing yourself without putting your partner on the defensive.

Your goal is to help your partner recognize why his actions have hurt you, particularly in the context of wounds from your early life. Therefore, take a step back and view the three issues that you choose from a wider and more objective perspective. Explaining why certain actions trigger you allows your partner to understand why you just can't get over them. It also limits your partner's desire to dismiss or minimize these incidents and your distress, and it increases the likelihood that he will apologize from the heart in a later e-mail.

Please use the following template exactly, inserting your own specifics. Here are some tips.

- Try not to use accusing "you" statements, like "you acted like I didn't even exist." Instead, use "I" statements, like "I felt unimportant."

- Try to use neutral, objective language—how you would describe the scene if you were watching a video of it. For example, "you walked out the door without saying goodbye" is fine, but "you were rude and stormed out" is not.

- Try your hardest to get inside your partner's head and empathize with her. The more true empathy you convey, the likelier your partner is to be open and not defensive when apologizing. Your partner was likely not trying to hurt you intentionally, so try to come up with other reasons why your partner may have acted as she did.

Dear _____,

When writing to you about how you've hurt me in the past, I feel _____. Here are three ways that you have hurt me recently, how they made me feel, why the situation triggered a strong reaction in me, and how I can try to empathize with why you did them.

1. Situation: _____

How I felt: _____

Why this triggered me: _____.

Why you may have acted as you did: _____.

2. Situation: _____

How I felt: _____

Why this triggered me: _____.

Why you may have acted as you did: _____.

3. Situation: _____

How I felt: _____

Why this triggered me: _____.

Why you may have acted as you did: _____.

Dear Zoe,

I feel sad writing to you about these situations, because I don't like to think back to all the times when I have felt hurt and betrayed. Who would? But I will try.

1. When you told my dad that I'm "not exactly killing myself" to make partner, that made me feel diminished and embarrassed. When I think back to my childhood, this is how I felt around my dad whenever I didn't bring home perfect grades. You probably were trying to joke around, or possibly you were trying to brag about how you are working hard yourself.

2. When you laughed when Elaine asked if we're going to get a dog, it made me feel insecure, since I thought it would happen soon. This triggered me because I used to feel similarly when my sister would tell me that she would hang out with me and then went back on her word. Worse, she would act like she had never promised at all. You probably laughed because it was a point of contention, and you always laugh when you're uncomfortable.

3. When you missed the window to book the hotel for our anniversary, it made me feel insecure too. I felt like if you cared more, you would have booked it early. I think this whole thing triggered me because my mom was always spacing out and doing things at the last minute, and, like with the hotel, things often went badly. Once she missed the deadline for applying to soccer camp, and then I couldn't go. You probably honestly have ADHD, which is why this stuff tends to happen.

Anyway, I am glad to have written this, because it makes me realize that maybe there is more than meets the eye to why I got so upset.

> I love you so much,
>
> Emily

Dear Emily,

I feel ambivalent about writing this e-mail, because I am mostly over these things, so it seems silly to bring them up. However, maybe thinking about them will be interesting and can help you understand me.

1. When you rejected me when I asked for sex last week and went right to sleep, I felt . . . rejected. This probably triggered me because nobody ever wanted to do anything with me when I was a kid. My brother was too cool, and my parents were working. It was me, myself, and I. When you turn over and go to sleep, I feel lonely, like I did then. To your credit, you were probably just tired, and I think you were getting a cold.

2. When you pushed me on the marriage thing in front of your sister, and the two of you were trying to prove to me that we should do it, I felt ambushed and blindsided. This was how I felt around my brother a lot. He was smarter and older, and he would twist my words and embarrass me. If I am being objective, you did this because you really want to get married and you saw a chance to persuade me.

3. When you called me a "robot," that hurt me. I try to be loving, but it's never enough. This triggers the feelings I had when I was little, when I felt I wasn't good enough for my brother. Objectively, in this case, I do think you were trying to hurt me, but I think it's because you felt hurt by me in some way (I don't remember what I did, but probably something that seemed cold?).

I love you,

Zoe

Apologies

27 Apologies

Now is the time to apologize to your partner for at least one of the issues that your partner shared with you in e-mail 26. This template allows you to write a meaningful apology that may finally make your partner feel validated and understood. If you want to apologize for two of the situations—or all three—that's bonus!

Dear _____,

When reading how you felt about _____, I felt _____. I will not make any excuses for how I behaved, but I would like you to understand the larger context for my actions. I think that how I acted is part of a larger pattern of acting _____. I learned this pattern early in life, from _____.

I try (or have not yet tried) to stop doing this, but I will try harder in the future. Here are two concrete ways in which I will try to stop myself from doing something similar.

I am sorry that _____.

Dear Violet,

When reading how you felt about me staying out all night without calling, I felt really bad. I will not make any excuses for how I behaved, but I would like you to understand the larger context for my actions. I think that how I acted is part of a larger pattern of acting like I shouldn't have to tell anyone what I'm doing or where I'm going. I learned this pattern early in life, when my parents didn't really care what I did, since they were never around much. I have not tried yet to stop doing this, but I will try in the future.

Here are two concrete ways in which I will try to stop myself from doing something similar: I will just call you, and I won't give you any attitude about it. I am sorry that I hurt you.

I love you,

Jeff

Dear Jeff,

When reading how you felt about me rejecting you in bed, I felt sad. I will not make any excuses for how I behaved, but I would like you to understand the larger context for my actions. I think that how I acted is part of a larger pattern of acting like sex isn't important or is annoying. I learned this pattern early in life, since I didn't see my mother date anyone, and she would always make comments about sex being bad and dangerous. I have tried to be more open about sex, and I will try harder in the future.

Here are two concrete ways that I will try to stop myself from doing something similar: I will be nicer if I am saying no, and I will try to initiate sex when I am feeling more in the mood.

I am sorry that I rejected you.

Your lovey,

Violet

28 Forgiveness

Here is a chance either to forgive your partner, accepting her apology in the previous e-mail, or to tell her how close you are to being able to forgive. You can explore what forgiveness means to you and how integral it is to the relationship you want to have moving forward. Forgiving does not mean forgetting, but some version of forgiveness or acceptance is essential to repairing trust and looking toward the future.

Use the first prompt, as well as at least three others, and end with two or three open-ended questions!

- Writing about forgiveness to you makes me feel _____.

- Here is what forgiveness means to me: _____.

- If I forgave you, I would feel _____.

- I forgive you (or do not forgive you) for [what was apologized for in the previous e-mail], because _____.

- I think (or do not think) it is possible for us to move forward and heal without forgiveness, because _____.

- It took me so long to forgive you because _____.

- I forgave you right away because _____.

- I will know I am ready to forgive you when _____.

- I witnessed (or did not witness) forgiveness at home growing up, and this impacted me in these ways: _____.

- I want (do not want) to model forgiveness for our children, because _____.

Dear Elaine,

I feel detached and distant as I write this. I do not yet forgive you for jeopardizing your life, as well as getting your license taken away. What if the kids had been in the car? You need help, and I don't think that you're getting it with your mandatory counseling. I know that because Mom never got straightened out until she committed to AA and went every single day. I will be able to forgive you when I know you are committing fully to the process of getting sober. I want to show a loving and forgiving relationship to our kids, but it would be BS for me to say I forgive you when I don't.

Questions:

- Will you go to AA?
- Will you go to rehab?

Love,

Barry

Dear Barry,

I feel nervous writing this, because I know you don't forgive me for the accident, nor should you. And I don't like to write about my own past grievances, because they seem petty next to what we are dealing with, but here goes: I have already forgiven you for how you acted when I slept at Mary's after the party. I understand you were worried. At the time, I felt that your reaction was crazy, and I thought you were jealous, and I now realize it was unrealistic for me to think that you would just assume that I lost my phone and was sleeping there. I also forgive you for asking my mom to talk to me about my drinking. I know you're worried. I want us to model forgiveness for our kids, and I hope you find it in your heart to love me again and to trust that I am done with drinking. I'm scared straight.

Questions:

- How long will it take before you forgive me?

- Is there anything I can do to regain your trust that doesn't involve going to AA?

I love you, and I'm sorry,

Elaine

CHAPTER 7

Childhood Issues

As we've discussed, your childhood and the relationships that you experienced and observed in your family directly shape your perspectives about relationships. For most couples, learning about each other's childhood facilitates empathy and understanding. In this chapter, you have the opportunity for introspection about your upbringing and how it affects your current relationship.

Couples are often uncomfortable delving into deeper childhood issues until they have built a foundation of trust and worked on more present-focused issues. The work you have done thus far in this book has primed you to open up in these e-mails. If you and your partner are in crisis, this may be the most essential and eye-opening chapter in this book.

29 Imago Theory

In *Getting the Love You Want*, Harville Hendrix discusses *imago theory*, which states that people tend to pick partners who remind them of their parents or primary caregivers at a deep, subconscious level.[4] That is, they choose an *imago*— (Latin for "image," "likeness," or "echo")—of their parents. In the honeymoon stage, you only see the positive similarities, but over time, your disillusionment leads you to focus on the negative similarities. Both partners' subconscious fantasy is to change the other in ways that they could never change their caregivers during childhood.

For example, imagine a girl who had a father with a great sense of humor and whom she loved very much. But she missed him greatly when he traveled for work, and she felt that she never had his full attention, even when he was home. Her unmet childhood need may have been consistent attention. Now, as a grown woman, she may subconsciously choose a partner who also makes her laugh but who is not entirely emotionally available. This man would be her imago, because he has the same positives and negatives as her dad.

During early courtship, she would likely only be conscious of the positives, but over time, the negatives would become more salient. At that point, she would likely try to change her partner in ways she could never change her dad, such as begging him to be more emotionally open, pushing him to commit before he is ready, and so forth. According to imago theory, this woman would likely not have fallen for a more emotionally open guy, because he would not be the ideal partner who triggers her love.

Imago theory applies to all people, even those who were raised in happy homes. No parents are perfect, and at times, every child feels that his needs aren't fully met. These unmet needs tend to form the basis for the imagined ideal partner later in life.

In this e-mail, you'll dig deep to think about similarities between your partner and your parents. Some will be qualities that make you feel loved and happy, and some will be qualities that make you feel insecure and upset. Try to be as neutral as possible when describing the negative qualities; your goal is not to insult your partner but to explore your relationship through a new lens.

Use all of these prompts and end with two or three open-ended questions!

- Writing this e-mail to you makes me feel _____.

- Here are the qualities you share with my mother (or father) that make me feel happy (or secure or full of admiration): _____.

- Here are the qualities that you share with my mother (or father) that make me feel unhappy (or insecure or critical): _____.

Dear Pauline,

I feel fine writing this e-mail to you. You share many qualities with my parents that are positive; you are smart, outgoing, and funny. You are also honest, which makes me feel secure, since it makes me confident that you'd never lie or cheat on me.

You also share a couple of negative ones with them: you don't like my career choice, and you push me to be more ambitious. But I guess those can be positive, since you do help me be a better person.

Questions:

- How am I like your parents?
- Do you think this imago idea has any validity?

I love you!

Louis

Dear Louis,

I feel sad writing this e-mail, because it makes me realize that there are qualities you share with my dad that make me upset. But first, the positives. You're like my mom in that you're social and friendly, and you're like my dad in that you're really into music. But you're also like my dad in that I don't know if you're going to have a secure job. This makes me feel anxious, because we want a family one day, so we'll need to be financially secure, and I don't want to be the sole breadwinner. I know you make some money with your music, but I don't think it's enough for us to count on. I loved my dad, but his lack of a consistent income was really hard on my family.

- Do you ever genuinely consider letting music become a hobby and finding something else?
- Are you offended by that question?

Love,

Pauline

30 Triggers

In this chapter, we will discuss your triggers—events, behaviors, topics, or places that elicit a strong reaction in you by forcing you to remember a particularly upsetting event from your past. You may be aware of your triggers, or you may have never thought about them. And most people are only vaguely aware of their partner's triggers, if they are aware of them at all.

It is imperative to understand your partner's triggers and to share your own, for two reasons. First, you don't want to unknowingly insult or tease each other about a hot-button issue, and second, you can use the information to bolster each other's self-esteem in areas of particular vulnerability.

For example, if a child grew up being teased excessively about being lazy, he may be sensitive to even gentle teasing about this issue. If a partner doesn't know the backstory, he may dismiss and invalidate his partner by calling this reaction "oversensitive." However, if this trigger is discussed, his partner can try to notice and praise his industriousness and competence, which would have a healing effect.

Use the first prompt, as well as at least three others, and end with two or three open-ended questions!

- Writing this e-mail makes me feel _____.

- Here are some issues I am sensitive about because of issues in my childhood or in previous relationships: _____.

- Here is how I feel when one of these issues is triggered: _____.

- Here is a recent time I felt triggered in my daily life, and how I reacted: _____.

- I have felt triggered when you've said or done this to me: _____.

- When discussing these sensitive issues, I would ideally like you to act this way: _____.

- I would like to act this way to you about your sensitive issues: _____.

- I would feel safer sharing my triggers with you if _____.

Dear Ariel,

I feel uncomfortable writing about this to you, because I haven't shared much about my relationship with my dad, except to say that it sucked and that he was unfailingly critical. One sensitive area for me is my weight. My dad would mock my weight and call me "Killer," which was short for "Killer Whale." He even explained this nickname to my first girlfriend, since I was dumb enough to bring her home. He also said I was stupider than my brother (do you like how he would insult both of us in one swoop?).

Recently, when you said I should lay off the birthday cake, I felt hurt. I know this might be surprising, since I laugh everything off, but it reminded me of how I felt around my father. I don't want to say you should never comment on my weight, but if you do, I would like it to be constructive feedback, not teasing in front of people, which is what Dad did.

Questions:

- How much weight do you think I should lose?
- Did your parents ever tease you?

Love,

Matt

Dear Matt,

I am uncomfortable writing to you about my triggers, because it's not something I think about. But the main issue that triggers me is when you come home late from hanging out with your friends, because my dad used to stay out all night. Even though you have never been out all night, I worry that you will start, especially now that your brother is single again and trying to party like he's twenty-five. I am also triggered by your drinking, because of how my dad acted when he was drunk. When I feel like you're even a little bit out of control, it makes me tense.

I have never explained this to you before because I never really acknowledged that you can remind me of my father. But when I thought about why the drinking and the staying out bother me, this answer seemed obvious.

- What are your triggers?
- Do you think I am being silly?

Love,

Ariel

31 Insecurities

In childhood and adolescence, most kids develop insecurities about aspects of themselves, including looks, personality, intellect, and the ability to attract friends and partners. It can help relationships greatly to learn the origin of each partner's insecurities. Otherwise, you run the risk of invalidating and dismissing each other, as insecurities often seem silly or unreal to those who don't understand their origin.

For example, if a man marries a beautiful and fit woman who constantly asks him if she looks okay, he may begin to feel annoyed and impatient or think that she's just fishing for compliments. But if he learned that she developed breasts earlier than the other girls in her grade, had braces, and was teased by the other kids for being ugly, he would have more compassion and patience when asked for reassurance.

Use the first prompt, as well as at least three others, and end with two or three open-ended questions!

- Writing to you about my childhood insecurities makes me feel _____.

- As a child (or preteen or teenager), I was most insecure about _____.

- Peers (or family members) used to tease me about _____.

- I reacted to being teased by _____.

- When you tease me about any of these issues, I feel _____.

Dear Ari,

I feel awkward and vulnerable writing this. I try not to think about that time in my life. As a child, I was most insecure about my parents being divorced. Before that, I genuinely don't remember feeling self-conscious about much. But when they split up, when I was eight, it started a cascade of insecurities about having less money and worse clothes than the other kids. Then in middle school, I was insecure about my skin and my teeth. The kids would tease me and call me Alvin (the chipmunk). In high school, I thought I would be the only girl without a boyfriend, and lo and behold, I was right.

In college, I dyed my hair and started acting more outgoing. That was a conscious decision; I think I was trying to be like Courtney Love or something. When we met, you said you thought I was really cool. That was funny, because I thought that you must have been way cooler than I was and that if we'd known each other in high school, you never would have talked to me.

- Do you have any childhood insecurities?
- What do you think of the stuff I told you?

Love,

Rebecca

Dear Rebecca,

I feel great writing to you about my childhood insecurities!
Just kidding. I feel embarrassed. As a kid, my main insecurity
was being Jonathan's brother, since my teachers were always
like, "*You're* Jonathan's brother?" They expected another child
prodigy, and they were sorely disappointed. I was insecure about
my intelligence and my academic achievement basically until . . .
now. I was also insecure about my prowess with the opposite sex
throughout middle school and high school. I still am! So when you
tease me sometimes about slobbering all over you when we kiss,
that makes me feel kind of bad, because that actually happened
once—a girl told me I was a bad kisser. Don't feel bad though; I
know you're not trying to hurt me. But I figured that this was the
kind of secret that we were going for in these e-mails.

Questions:

- How bad of a kisser do you think I am?

- Do you think I'm smart?

- Am I just fishing for compliments here?

Te amo, mi amor,

Ari

CHAPTER 8

Let's E-mail About Sex

If you're like many couples, it's unlikely that you have had many honest, face-to-face discussions about sex. It's a shame this topic is so difficult to discuss openly, because sex and eroticism are integral parts of a healthy and connected relationship.

Sexual difficulties can occur in otherwise fulfilling relationships. Even if everything else is great, your sex life may feel stale, disconnected, or unsatisfying. Sometimes your emotional connection has eroded, which has prevented you from connecting sexually. Even if your sexual relationship is satisfying, most couples find that reinvigorating their erotic connection is necessary from time to time.

In this chapter, you'll be guided through e-mailing your partner about your thoughts and feelings about sex. Since you are writing this e-mail privately, you don't have to worry about hearing a shocked gasp or a disapproving look. Your focus should be on reflecting about your personal experiences, thoughts, and feelings about sex, and communicating these openly to your partner.

32 What Did I Learn About Sex Growing Up?

Your attitudes toward sex and your sexual identity start being shaped much earlier than your first sexual relationship. Childhood provides you with your earliest instruction about sex, and what you observe at that critical time can influence your adult desires, predilections, and inhibitions. Understanding the origin of your unique sexuality and sharing this insight with your partner can be enlightening and enriching for your relationship.

Children who were not exposed to healthy, positive, and open discussions about sex can have many issues in adulthood. They may have inhibitions surrounding physical affection, pass judgment about sexual practices that don't seem "normal," or may feel detached or distant during sex. On the flip side, others become promiscuous or base their identity on their sexuality and attractiveness.

The physical relationship that you witnessed between your parents can provide clues as to why you may feel as you do about physical intimacy and affection. Partners often have different ideas about how much physical affection is expected or desired on a daily basis, and the roots of this disparity can be found in the relationships that they observed growing up. If a partner has considered you uptight or hypersexual, this e-mail can foster empathy by providing a window into why you may act as you do.

Use the first prompt, as well as at least three others, and end with two or three open-ended questions!

- Discussing our sex life makes me feel _____.

- Here is what my mother and my father told me about sex, both outright and what they implied: _____.

- My earliest thoughts about sex were _____.

- Physical affection in my house was like this: _____.

- This is what my mother and father's sexual relationship may have been like: _____.

- As a child, I was curious about _____.

- The healthiest physical relationship that I observed as a child was between _____.

- The most important things I'd want to teach my (or our) kids about sex are _____.

Dear Alexis,

This is a weird e-mail for me to write, since I think it's strange to be discussing my parents' sex life, but I'm game. To be honest, my parents were weird about sex, and since we've had kids, I have thought a lot about how they acted. I never remember seeing my parents touch except for a peck on the lips. Once I overheard my mother telling my aunt that she couldn't wait till Dad travelled for work, and I had the impression that it was about her not wanting to have sex with him. I don't know why I thought that, maybe there is more to the story that I don't remember. It made me feel embarrassed and sad. I wished that my parents seemed happier.

I remembering seeing my cousin Martin and his girlfriend making out when he brought her home from college. Then he married her—she was his first wife. I was a kid then, and I remember wanting to be just like him when I grew up. Maybe that is why I am always "all over you." I remember that made a big impression on me, that two people would be so open about being attracted to each other. I wondered what their sex life was like. Maybe I should ask him now! Ha.

I want to raise our kids seeing us hug, kiss, and even make out all the time. I will try not to be "all over you" and grope you and stuff, but maybe now you see where it comes from.

Love you,

Josh

Dear Josh,

I feel happy writing you this e-mail, because I have thought a lot about this topic, and I think it is an area where we do really well. When I was married to John, the kids didn't see a lot of affection, and that made me upset. When you and I got together, our physical connection was more like what I remember seeing between my parents, a lot of touching and cuddling and hugging. I am glad that our kids see us doing that, although I would, of course, also like them to see less fighting.

My earliest thought about sex was that it was disgusting. I wanted to know if people could still be married without doing it. My friend had told me about penises going into vaginas, and I thought that was gross. I asked my mom, and she said that it is wonderful when people love each other. As I got older, I started to realize that when my parents went into their room on Sunday afternoons, that's what they were probably doing. I asked my sister, and she said, "Yeah, dummy." So from about ten years old on, I thought that sex was good between people who loved each other, and I still agree with that! I hope we can work out our other issues, because I have always loved being intimate with you.

My questions:

- Does our fighting impact how much you want to have sex with me, like it does for me?

- Are you happy with the amount of affection we show to the kids?

I love you,

Alexis

33 My Sexual History

Many couples believe that "don't ask, don't tell" is the healthiest policy for discussing their sexual history. Couples assume that they will be racked with jealousy upon hearing what a partner enjoyed with a previous lover. For many people, however, especially those feeling bored with their current sex life, hearing about a partner's prior experiences can rekindle a spark.

It can also be educational to hear what a partner's earliest sexual experiences entailed. Reading about your partner's first encounters can shed new light on her unique preferences. It is good practice to start out less detailed and ask your partner if she wants you to expand. Some partners will not, and some, possibly surprisingly to you, will want to hear specifics. You don't have to elaborate on details if you're uncomfortable, and certainly not if you suspect that your partner is trying to use your past against you ("Wait, you went down on him, but you won't go down on me?"). If your partner seems interested, however, try to be open about your memories and history. Visualizing your partner as a sexual and romantic being prior to your relationship can often be reinvigorating, and moderate jealousy is actually an adaptive emotion, as it leads to mate-guarding and ensuring that a partner doesn't just run off with someone else.

Use the first prompt, as well as at least three others, and end with two or three open-ended questions!

- Telling you about my sexual history makes me feel _____.

- My first time having sex (or oral sex) was _____.

- My first time touching another person sexually was _____.

- The first time I felt sexually excited was _____.

- Here's what I thought about my first sexual experience: _____.

- I first started to enjoy sex when _____.

- My earliest sexual fantasy was _____.

- The trait that I am most sexually attracted to in men (or women) is _____.

- The common theme among people that I am attracted to is _____.

- I first started masturbating when I was _____ years old, and what I thought about was _____.

- This is how I feel about how many people I've been sexual with _____.

- An exciting sexual experience that I had as a teenager (or as a young adult or before meeting you) was _____.

- The first person I felt sexual feelings for was _____.

- My first orgasm was _____.

- The similarities between you and the people I was attracted to in my early life are _____.

Dear Jen,

I'm leery about writing you this e-mail. Some of this stuff we've discussed before, and some we haven't. I'm worried that you won't want to respond to me, since I've tried to bring this stuff up with you before, and you've said that you don't really want to know about my history and that you have "nothing much to tell." I'm also worried that you're going to be jealous or mad when you hear about things I did with other women, but you want me to be open to writing these e-mails, so I will try.

The first woman I was attracted to that I remember was She-Ra on television, when I was a kid. But the first real person was my second-grade teacher. I also always had a crush on someone in every class I was in from kindergarten on. What can I say? I loved the ladies. I think the common theme was that the women were nice and had an hourglass shape, like you.

My first orgasm was at age eleven or so, when masturbating. I thought about girls from school and my sister's friends. I was addicted to masturbating throughout my teen years and probably through college. Once or twice a day every day.

My questions are:

- Do you still masturbate, and how often?
- When did you start to enjoy sex, and with whom?
- What was your first really exciting sexual experience?
- What, exactly, did you do with your first boyfriend?

(Sorry that was four, but you know you never answer me on this stuff, and I'm curious.) I love you, and I hope you liked my e-mail, and I hope you'll write back soon!

Yours,

Paul

Dear Paul,

I am shy about telling you about my sexual history, because it's awkward and new for us. But maybe it will bring us closer, especially since you always want to know this stuff. I'm also anxious that I'm going to hear things that I don't want to know about your past. I know I am not as wild as other women you were with, and I am scared that I might find out that they were even crazier than I imagine.

The first time I had sex was with my boyfriend when I was sixteen. He turned out to be a jerk, and I didn't enjoy the sex. But I did enjoy making out with him, and the first orgasm I had was dry humping with him. The very first sexual feelings I felt were toward my junior high school boyfriend (but we only kissed) and toward camp counselors I thought were cute, when I was a camper. I didn't think of these feelings as sexual at the time, but in retrospect, they were.

I first enjoyed sex in college, but I didn't orgasm from sex then. I didn't orgasm from sex until you.

My questions:

- When did you first orgasm with a partner?

- Were you sexually attracted to me at first, or did you first think of me as just a friend?

- Do you wish that I had had more partners or was more experienced?

I love you,

Jen

34 What I Love That We Do

Here is an opportunity to shower your partner with positive feedback about your sex life. This may be difficult if you haven't had good sex—or any sex—for a while. However, if you think back, it is likely that many of your early encounters were exciting. If not, focus on an aspect that you do or did find erotic, such as kissing, touching, or the way that your partner looks, sounds, or smells.

If your sexual relationship is fulfilling, don't feel shy about enthusiastically praising it! This is a gift to your partner. He may not be confident that you're enjoying yourself, if you're not a big talker, so this is a chance to provide some reassurance and stroke his ego.

Many people have no idea which features of their sex life are most exciting or pleasurable to their partners, as they never get open and concrete feedback or suggestions. But once they know what a partner likes, they can do more of it.

Use the first prompt, as well as at least three others, and end with two or three open-ended questions!

- Discussing our sex life with you makes me feel _____.

- My favorite thing that you do in bed is _____.

- Something wonderful that you do that no other partner ever did is _____.

- Here is how I feel about your looks: _____.

- My favorite sexual experience that I ever had with you was _____.

- The last sex dream I had about you was _____.

- I am most attracted to you when _____.

- The moment I was most excited in our first sexual encounter was _____.

- The moment I was most excited in our most recent sexual encounter was _____.

- You are particularly sexually talented at _____.

- When I fantasize about you, I think about the time that _____.

Dear Todd,

I feel okay about writing this e-mail. Sex has been a good part of our relationship over the years, although lately, when we have been more distant in other ways, I have found myself wondering if you just want me for sex.

You are particularly talented at kissing. I always like making out with you, and I wish we took more time kissing before getting to the main event. Of course, it's tough with kids around, but still.

I have always thought you are handsome, and I am glad you're still in shape. A lot of my friends' husbands have gained weight, and I feel good that you still run and lift weights.

I am most attracted to you when we have just had a real conversation, not about the kids' schedules or other day-to-day stuff, but about something meaningful. Also, when you just get back from working out.

My questions:

> If I couldn't have sex with you for a year because I got sick or something, would you stay faithful?

- Do you miss how we used to make out for hours?

XOXO,

Liza

Dear Liza,

I feel awesome writing you this e-mail, because finally there is one that comes easy to me! I am so attracted to you, and I always have been. No matter what ups and downs our marriage goes through, I always lust after you, and you know that.

My favorite thing that you do in bed is oral sex. You're awesome at that, and I feel great that a lot of guys say they don't get oral after marriage, but I still do. You're the best.

The most exciting moment in our first sexual encounter was when you asked me if I had a condom. I wasn't expecting us to have sex right then, although I was prepared on the off chance! The second most exciting moment was when you came. I felt awesome about that, because I was worried that you weren't going to be into it. Possibly since I was a little drunk too (ha!).

The most exciting moment in our most recent sexual encounter was when you turned over. You know I like to do it from behind, and you're so sexy.

Questions:

- What are your favorite things we do in bed?

- When did you first know you wanted to have sex with me the first time?

- Do you still like giving oral, or is it a chore?

Love,

Todd

35 My Sex Drive

There are many explanations for variability in sex drives, including hormonal issues, lack of novelty in a monogamous relationship (which I call *monotogamy*), body-image issues, medications, mental health issues, and marital conflict. It is unlikely that both partners will have similar sex drives once the honeymoon stage is over. Often, differences in sex drive can lead to explosive conflict. Both partners feel that their rights are being infringed upon: the partner with a lower sex drive feels coerced into sex, and the other partner feels cut off from an activity that brings pleasure, joy, and connection.

Partners of both genders can feel rejected and unloved when they are continually turned down for sex. Men are generally taught that their virility is an integral part of their identity and that men in monogamous relationships should have sex as frequently as they want to. Women with higher sex drives than their male partners can feel even worse, since society assumes that women are always pursued for sex by their male partners.

Talking about your and your partner's sex drives can be illuminating. If your drives are mismatched, you can learn to act as a team—the two of you versus the mismatched sex drive. This can happen only if you understand and empathize with one another, which comes from open discussion.

Use the first prompt, as well as at least three others, and end with two or three open-ended questions!

- Discussing my sex drive with you makes me feel _____.

- I think my sex drive changed since we first met in this way: _____.

- I wish my sex drive was higher (or lower), because _____.

- I have always thought my sex drive was higher (or lower) than other people's, and this makes me feel _____.

- Here is how stress (or medication, hormonal changes, relationship conflicts, or body-image issues) impacts my sex drive: _____.

- When you complain about me wanting too much (or not enough) sex, I feel _____.

- Some ways that we could cope better with our mismatched sex drives are _____.

Dear Lauren,

This is a hard e-mail for me to write, because I know this is a sensitive topic for you. I know we are not in the usual situation, the one your friends are in, with their husbands wanting sex every minute. Things have gotten worse since I started Prozac. I thought we were pretty well matched before, but since I got depressed and then since I started meds, your sex drive is way higher than mine.

I wish my sex drive were higher. It makes me feel terrible that you think I don't want you. I do find you very attractive physically, but it is hard to concentrate on sex when I am feeling down, and now—with the meds—I just can't come as easily. I hope that things change; maybe I can find a different medication. I just don't want to change my meds yet, because my mental health is precarious as it is. Maybe in a few months.

I think that watching porn together would help with my sex drive, but I know how you feel about that. I have read that people on meds may need more stimulation to orgasm, and that's what watching porn would do. But I understand if you don't want to.

My questions:

- Do you believe me when I say I think you're hot, even though I don't always want to have sex?

- Are you going to leave me for some guy who wants to have sex 24/7?

- Do you regret marrying me?

Yours,

John

Dear John,

I am angry and resentful writing about this. I am trying hard not to feel that way, but our sex life has been a sore subject for a long time. I understand about your meds, but you don't understand just how rejected and awful I feel. It makes me feel like a fool that my friends' husbands chase them down for sex, and my own husband would rather play Scrabble.

I don't think you realize that sometimes, when I want to have sex, it's actually because I feel insecure about myself. I've gained weight since the kids, and I want to know—really know—that you still find me attractive. All the compliments in the world don't help if you don't want to touch me. So my body-image issues actually *increase* my sex drive, I guess. So does relationship conflict. If we're fighting, I want to make up by having passionate sex, not just talking endlessly.

I have always thought my sex drive was higher than other women's, and I remember my ex-boyfriend saying how I wore him out. But it was a positive thing. I entered this marriage knowing that you weren't as high as me in the sex-drive department, but we were closer than now.

I love you, and I want to make this work. As I have said before, maybe we can see if there are other meds that work for you.

Questions:

- Will you consult with Dr. Smith about changing your Prozac to something else?

- Would you continue with this once-a-month sex forever?

Love,

Lauren

36 ♥ What I'm Curious About

In individual therapy, many people mention wanting to try things in bed that they believe that their partner would never try, and they feel that their partners would judge them negatively for even wanting such things. Thinking that your partner would condemn your deepest sexual desires can make you feel lonely and sad. This imagined or real judgment from a partner echoes the judgmental attitude about sexuality that many individuals felt at home as children or teenagers.

Expressing sexual fantasies to a partner is one of the most intimate and vulnerable things that you can do. Many people have never discussed sexual fantasies before, and they think about these fantasies only when they are masturbating or having sex. Confiding these most intimate and personal thoughts to your partner can be incredibly erotic.

Both partners should realize that writing or receiving this e-mail does not represent an agreement to engage in these fantasy activities. If you're writing about your fantasies in order to coerce or guilt-trip your partner into doing an activity against her will, this will erode the closeness that you're trying to cultivate.

Similarly, don't use your partner's e-mail against her. Sharing secret sexual thoughts and fantasies makes people feel vulnerable, and your partner is trusting that you will not mock or belittle her fantasies. Also, don't ask, "Is that all?" when your partner expresses herself. Some people's fantasies seem low-key compared to others', but this does not make them less difficult to share openly.

Use the first prompt, as well as at least three others, and end with two or three open-ended questions!

- Writing to you about what I'm sexually curious about makes me feel _____.

- Here are the top three things I would like to try in bed that I have never tried with you: _____.

- Something I have always wanted us to do *again* is _____.

- Something that I have fantasized about since my earliest memories is _____.

- My favorite sexual fantasy is _____.

- A movie or book that turns me on is _____.

- I am scared to tell you that I am curious about _____.

- Here is how I feel about the following (pick any of these): _____.

  - group sex
  - fantasies about rape or taking someone by force
  - using toys in the bedroom
  - watching porn together

- reading erotic stories together
- public sex
- bondage or domination
- spanking
- oral sex
- anal sex
- teasing or denial
- quickies

- I am curious about orgasming in this way: _____.

- The craziest thing that I find exciting is _____.

- You would never guess that I have wondered about _____.

- I have never told anyone else that I am curious about _____.

- One time, I was about to tell you that I like _____, but I chickened out.

- When you don't want to try things that I like, I feel _____.

- When I think that I may never do some of my fantasies in real life, I feel _____.

- The fantasy that would most disappoint me if it never happened is _____.

Dear Marie,

I'm excited to write this e-mail to you, because you have to write the same one back! I really want to see what you write. Most of my e-mail is stuff I've already told you, but I will try and put myself out there and tell you some new things.

The top three things I would like to try are anal, a threesome, and 69. I know how you feel about these things, but I still hold out hope. I would not like to go to my grave having not tried anal sex or 69. The threesome is more of a fantasy (unless you want to!). I have wanted to try anal since I was a teenager, when I saw it in a porno. That is, to be honest, my go-to fantasy.

One time I was going to tell you that I was curious about going to an adults-only resort, but I chickened out. I am sure that would not be your scene, and maybe it wouldn't really be mine either.

When you don't want to try things I like, I feel rejected. Usually I just withdraw, like we talked about me doing in other areas of the marriage. Early on, I felt that these things would be so easy for you, and I just couldn't understand why you wouldn't try. Over time, however, I have started to realize that you love me but you find it really hard to try these things. I understand that, but I will honestly tell you that I still feel rejected and hurt.

My questions for you:

- Do you think our sex life is exciting enough?
- What is your favorite sexual fantasy?
- Do you secretly think anal is gross, or is it just that you think it would hurt, like you say?

Love,

Liam

Dear Liam,

I am super anxious to write to you about what I am sexually curious about, because, to be honest, I am scared that you will instantly want to try everything on the list. Right now I am so exhausted with the kids that I barely feel like having sex at all, so this e-mail isn't saying that I want to do everything on the list. I am taking a leap of faith that writing this will make us feel closer, but—just to tell you in advance—I *don't* want to try everything on it, at least not right now. (Sorry!)

One thing I have been curious about is using a vibrator again. We tried it when we got married, and I said I didn't like it, but now that my sex drive is lower because of nursing, it might be a good way to get me closer to orgasm, so we could finish together.

I also am curious about spanking, which is something you have tried, but you probably thought I wasn't into it. I am into it! But—since kids—it makes me anxious to do anything too loud. So on a night when my mom has the kids?

My questions are:

- How do you feel about my e-mail?

- Were you expecting something more wild, and are you disappointed?

I love you,

Marie

CHAPTER 9

Parenting

Whether your children are newborns, teenagers, out of the house, or haven't even been born yet, the impact of kids on a relationship cannot be overstated. Often, couples get along well until a baby is born (or conceived), and then one or both partners become dissatisfied. This can be due to massive changes in the couple's day-to-day life, a mismatch between partners' expectations of each parent's role, the focus shifting from the couple to the family, a decrease in sex or couple time, hormonal changes, fatigue, new financial worries, or many other reasons.

When couples have similar values and priorities about parenting, it can be a great source of comfort and compatibility. However, parents with diverging views may argue frequently and grow disconnected, angry, and resentful. Other issues can fade in importance when compared to the stress of raising children, which often gets worse during the phases of toddlerhood and adolescence.

In this chapter, you'll have the opportunity to reflect on your hopes and fears about parenting, including your identity as a parent, the give-and-take between your roles as parent and as partner, your feelings about your family, and previously undisclosed thoughts about parenting.

If you and your partner are both committed to not having children, you can just skip much of this chapter, unless one or both of you would like to exchange e-mails about how you arrived at that decision. Some of the subjects in this chapter will be useful even for those who don't want to have children, such as e-mail 37, about your parents' parenting style.

37 My Parents' Parenting

In this e-mail, you will explore how your own mother and father (or other primary caregivers) shaped you, and in what respects you want to be both similar to and different from each parent. This information can help your partner understand you in a new way and visualize how your parents acted when you were young, which is often different than they act now.

As a bonus, this e-mail can help you clarify why certain aspects of parenting are so important to you and why you have chosen your current parenting style. This insight and introspection can help you become a more effective parent.

Use the first prompt, as well as at least three others, and end with two or three open-ended questions!

- Writing to you about parenting makes me feel _____.

- When I was young, these were three of my parents' strengths (or weaknesses) as parents: _____.

- Here are a few ways in which I want to raise our children the same way as (or differently from) I was raised: _____.

- When I was growing up, three words that described our family were: _____.

- Three words that currently describe my family with you are: _____.

- Three words that I would like to describe my family with you in the future are: _____.

- My parents' parenting style made me feel _____.

- In retrospect, I think that my parents acted the way they did because _____.

- When thinking back about my own childhood, I feel _____.

- I am worried (confident) about my own parenting, because I feel I will tend to resemble my parents in this way: _____.

- I am sad that I have repeated my parents' mistakes with our kids in this way: _____.

Dear Anne,

I feel angry writing about this topic, because I feel that I have done a lot of work to overcome my upbringing, but talking about it still riles me up. When I was young, my mother's strengths were being social, keeping a clean house, and training us to be polite. Her weaknesses were being verbally abusive, having a horrible temper, and playing favorites.

I don't want to take much from my mother's book. I do want to raise our kids with manners, but not at the expense of them feeling that they are accepted and loved. Her parenting style made me feel like a piece of garbage, not worthy of her attention or consideration.

In retrospect, my mom had a hard life, and she was doing the best she could, but I am still angry and resentful. I hope that I am a better parent than she was, and I know you'll be the mom to our kids that I would have always wished for myself.

Questions:

- Do you wish you married someone with normal parents?
- Are you anxious that I am going to be a crap dad, since I didn't even have one?

Love,

Drew

Dear Drew,

I feel okay about writing you this e-mail. I know you had a tough childhood, and sometimes I feel guilty that mine was pretty good. I also feel guilty if I complain, since your mom was so bad. You never make me feel that way, but I still do.

Three words that described my family were close, fun, and happy. I would like our own family to be the same. My mother's strengths were that she was laid back, creative, and loving. Her weaknesses were organization, time management, and taking on too much (e.g., the foster dogs, babysitting other kids). My dad's strengths were his sense of humor, his ability to befriend anyone, and his love of sports, which he passed on to all of us. His weaknesses were his lack of formal education (I didn't think it was a weakness, but he did), his drinking, and being a pushover, especially with the younger kids. Also, he let my mom do whatever she wanted to, even when it put the family under stress (like the foster dogs).

Questions:

- Do you think I can't understand you because I didn't grow up like you did?

- Do you like that I talk to your mom, or do you wish I didn't talk to her as much?

- When we have kids, do you think your mom is going to be a good grandmother?

All my love,

Anne

38 My Thoughts About Kids

Here you will have the opportunity to talk to your partner in depth about having children. If you're in a relatively new relationship, this may be an unexplored topic, and if you already have kids, this e-mail can bring you back to the first days of parenthood. Either way, this e-mail can bring you and your partner closer together by sharing your most personal thoughts about parenting.

- Writing you this e-mail makes me feel _____.

- Here is what I always felt about having kids when I was a kid myself: _____.

- Here is how I felt about having kids around the time that we started dating: _____ .

- Here is how I feel about having kids with you one day: _____.

- Here is what scares me about having kids: _____.

- Here is what I look forward to about having kids: _____.

- I decided to have kids with you when _____.

- This is how I felt when we got pregnant: _____.

- This is how I felt about our relationship during the pregnancy: _____.

- This is how I felt when I/you miscarried: _____.

- This is how I felt about our relationship when we had our first (or second or next) baby: _____.

- Having kids changed our relationship in these positive (or negative) ways: _____.

- Here is how I feel we are balancing parenting and couplehood: _____.

Dear Marianna,

This is a complicated e-mail for me to write. No matter what else we struggle with, I know you're a great mom and the only woman I would want to mother my children. However, as you know, having kids changed our relationship a great deal. I never would wish our kids away, of course, but I sometimes wish we had waited longer or spaced them out more—or anything that could have put us on a less child-centered path.

When I was a kid, I never thought much about having kids. My parents made jokes about how having kids ruined their lives, and at the time, I thought that they were funny. Only when we had kids ourselves did I realize that they shouldn't have said those things in front of us. I first really wanted kids when we got married. You wanted them so much, and I saw how great you were with Alexa, more like a mom than an aunt. I got excited to start a big, happy family with you.

I feel that we do have a big, happy family, but I don't feel like we're a couple now, between the kids in the bed and the constant stream of activities. I also feel lonely, and I don't think you do. The kids' love fills you up, but it isn't the same for me. I am hoping that through this book and maybe even counseling, we can get back to where we were eight years ago. Wow, that's such a long time!

Questions:

- Do you think if we got a babysitter ten or twenty hours a week it could take some stress off you and give us some time to be together?
- Do you even want time without the kids?

I love you,

Ryan

Dear Ryan,

I am happy writing you this e-mail, because I love our family and the life we have built for our kids. Growing up, I always wanted kids, probably because I wanted to raise them differently from how I was raised. My sister feels the same way, which is why she never considered putting Alexa up for adoption. When I met you, I knew you'd be a great dad, and that made me love you even more.

When we found out that I was pregnant, I was thrilled. Both times, but especially with Kayla. It was all so exciting, and you were so loving. Unfortunately, I think our marriage took a back seat to parenting for a while, especially when Colin was born. But now I feel that we are back on track, and compared to my friends, we are doing pretty well. We spend a lot of time together as a family, and our kids always see us working together as a team.

My questions:

- How did you *really* feel when I got pregnant with our little surprise?

- Do you ever think we should have a third?

- Do you think we should consider moving closer to my sister, so she and Alexa can be more of a part of our lives?

Love, love, love,

Marianna

39 Who Am I (or Who Will I Be) As a Parent?

This e-mail gives you the opportunity to reflect upon your identity as a mother or father. If you're already a parent, you can share what you're proud of and what you want to work on in the future. If you're not a parent yet, you can think about what type of parent you want to be someday, a topic that more couples would benefit from discussing. Either way, this is a discussion that can bring you and your partner much closer.

Use the first prompt, as well as at least three others, and end with two or three open-ended questions!

- Writing this e-mail to you makes me feel _____.

- Three words that describe who I hope to be as a parent are _____.

- Three words that describe who I currently am as a parent are _____.

- The top three things that I do well as a parent are _____.

- The top three things I want to work on as a parent are _____.

- One issue that gets in the way of me being the best parent I can be is _____.

- Here is how my parenting is affected by the following:
  - relationship conflict
  - stress
  - fatigue
  - work
  - emotional or mental health issues
  - the involvement of my (or your) family members

Dear Sal,

I feel sad and regretful writing this e-mail. My relationship with Sophie was fine until last year, and now I feel like I'm floundering as a mom. It is triggering my sadness about my relationship with my own mom. The top things I want to work on are patience, tolerance, and affection. It is hard for me to be patient when Sophie slacks off with schoolwork, and I know I am judgmental about Todd, even though I guess he's not the worst boyfriend she could have picked. Also, I find it hard to approach her to hug or kiss her nowadays, because I just feel angry all the time.

My parenting is impacted by the stress I'm under at work and by how tired I feel. I think menopause is on the horizon, and my PMS has been killer recently. I'm going to try to work on my own physical and emotional health, and hopefully that will improve my mindset and relationship with Soph.

Questions:

- Do you think she still loves me?

- Do you think it will get better or worse when she's out of the house next year?

I love you forever,

Kerri

Dear Kerri,

I feel happy writing this e-mail. I know I'm not a perfect parent, but compared to my own dad, I think I'm pretty good. I think three words that describe me as a parent are *patient*, *loving*, and *fun*. My strengths are keeping calm, being reasonable, and also playing sports with her.

I think I need to work on being able to talk to Sophie about sensitive, emotional stuff, which I usually just leave to you. And I want to make sure that I'm not working too much during her last year at home.

Questions:

- Do you think your issues with Sophie stem from you guys being too alike?

- Do you think I'm a good dad?

- Are you looking forward to her being out of the house at all?

Yours,

Sal

Your Parenting Strengths

Now is the time to share your thoughts about your partner's parenting strengths. Many people say things like "you're a good dad" without elaborating on what it means. Your partner will love hearing exactly what you think makes him an excellent parent, in detail. You may not think that your partner is the best possible parent, but this is a time to focus on the positive and share your warmest thoughts about the effort your partner puts in to raising your kids.

Use the first prompt, as well as at least three others, and end with two or three open-ended questions!

- Writing about your parenting strengths makes me feel _____.

- As a parent, I think you'll be _____.

- When deciding to be with you, your potential parenting strengths played this role: _____.

- It is important to me to be with someone who is similar to (or different from) my own parents in these ways: _____.

- Your top three parenting strengths are _____.

- Three things you're better at as a parent than I am are _____.

- The positive qualities that the kids notice in you are _____.

- A recent time when I was impressed with your parenting was when _____.

- Whenever I see you do _____ with the kids, I feel happy.

- Three ways you're helping me be the best parent I can be are _____.

- Here are some ways you're giving our kids a better childhood than I had: _____.

- Here are some ways that you have overcome your own difficult childhood to give our kids a better life: _____.

Dear Leo,

I feel great writing to you about your parenting strengths. When I first met you, I knew you'd be a great father. I thought you would be gentle, kind, and involved. I was right. Our children often treat you as the primary caretaker, which is evidence that they are happy and secure with you. You are more patient and more reliable than I am, and you show greater enthusiasm for the children's often-boring stories and activities. Whenever I see you take the kids outside to play, I feel happy.

I think that the children recognize that you are a loving and stable presence, and I am proud of myself for marrying you and giving that type of dad to my kids. My own father tried his best, but he had his mental health issues, so he wasn't really involved. You are very different from him, and that is why the children feel so comfortable around you. I think you are a much better parent than I am.

Questions:

- Do you think my parenting has improved since I have started taking my medication?

- Have I disappointed you as a mom to the kids?

Love,

Sarah

Dear Sarah,

I feel nice writing to you about your parenting. I always thought you would be a great mom, and I was right. With the exception of your temper, I think you are a wonderful mother to the kids. They know that you make the rules, and you teach them discipline. You come up with interesting projects and activities, and you are the driving force behind most things that we do on the weekends. The children love you and want your approval. I feel happy when I see you bathing the little guy or reading to the girls.

Unlike how I felt as a child, the kids can always count on you to know what's going on at school, to make sure they go to activities, and to give your all to the family.

You help me be a better parent by teaching me to be more emotionally aware and to talk to the girls about their feelings.

Questions:

- What do you think your easiest parenting stage was or will be?

- Do you think the girls will continue to be close to me as they become teenagers?

> I love you, my darling,
>
> Leo

41 Ways You Could Help Me Be a Better Parent

In this e-mail, you have the opportunity to explain how your partner could better support you as a parent. This is also the place where you can discuss your disappointments with some aspects of your partner's parenting. This is not the place for judgment or attacks. Instead, first admit your own weaknesses as a parent, and then focus on how your own parenting could be improved if your partner changed certain behaviors.

Try your hardest to steer clear of accusations. Use neutral language, and focus on what your partner could do in the future rather than on how she has disappointed you in the past.

Use the first prompt, as well as at least three others, and end with two or three open-ended questions!

- Writing on this topic to you makes me feel _____.

- Three ways that you could help me be a better partner are _____.

- Three things that you unintentionally do that hinder my ability to parent well are _____.

- Some ways that you could support me or affirm me as a parent are _____.

- Here are things I would love to hear you to say to me, which would make me more confident in my parenting: _____.
- Some ways that I could help you be a better parent are _____.

Dear Rachel,

I feel anxious about writing on this topic to you, because I am worried that you'll take offense. I understand that you feel that I could be more involved as a dad. But I feel that I am doing an okay job, especially given my work constraints. I am trying to work fewer weekends, and I do try to be involved in the evenings and on the weekends when I am home.

Ways you could help me be a better parent are not criticizing how much I work in front of the kids and your family, not telling me that I am doing things wrong with the baby, and allowing me to give some input into our family activities and plans.

I think that because I am not around as much as you'd want, you create a life without me, based only on your schedule and your plans. This makes me feel excluded and, ironically, makes me want to spend more time at work, since I feel like an outsider at home.

I would really appreciate your telling me sometimes that I am a good dad, particularly given that I am stumbling around blind here, having not had a dad for the majority of my life.

Questions:

- Do you consciously exclude my desires from our weekend plans?

- Do you think I am doing an okay job at all as a dad?

Love,

Oliver

Dear Oliver,

This is a hard e-mail for me to write, because I feel so conflicted. On one hand, I recognize that, in your mind, it is important for you to provide for us financially, and I know that you are doing the best you can to balance work and family. But that is not enough for me, and I am lonely and feel overwhelmed.

You could make me a better parent just by being around more. I have told you that I am willing for you to take a pay cut, for us to move somewhere where the lifestyle and expectations are different, or even for us to move closer to your job to reduce your commute. I am struggling with parenting on my own for twelve hours a day and on many weekends. I snap at the kids and feel exhausted all of the time. When you are around, I snap at you too, just like my mom used to do to my dad, and I am disappointed both in myself and in this marriage when that happens.

Questions:

- Why can't you commit to being around more, even if we moved closer to work?

- Do you miss me and the kids when you're at work?

- How many more years do you think your schedule will be like this?

Love,

Rachel

42 Similarities and Differences Between Me and My Parents

Many people imagine that they have chosen their own paths and developed their own preferences and values without much influence from their parents. As a therapist, I think of things differently. Most people tend to be divided into two camps: those who want to emulate their parents and those who don't. The first group loves to draw similarities between themselves and their parents, and the second group emphasizes the differences. However, all people share some similarities with their parents and have some differences, and it can be enlightening to explore both. When considering these similarities, aim for deep rather than superficial ones, such as values, goals, parenting styles, spirituality, relationships with spouses, relationships with friends, and so forth.

This may be the first time that you've considered the deep impact that your parents' values and choices have on your current identity, so take your time with this e-mail. Thinking through this carefully will allow both you and your partner to gain as much insight as possible into the impact of your background on your current conscious and subconscious life choices.

Use the first prompt, as well as at least three others, and end with two or three open-ended questions!

- Writing this e-mail to you makes me feel _____.

- The idea of having similarities with my parents makes me feel _____.

- The main similarities I share with my parents are _____.

- The ways I am different from my parents are _____.

- I want (or don't want) to resemble my parents in this way: _____.

- One thing I am glad I learned from my childhood is _____.

Dear Lorrie,

I feel happy writing you this e-mail, because it can help me express why I am so set on certain ways of parenting Claire. The main similarities I have with my parents are the value of being kind to others, a strong work ethic, and a commitment to social justice. I am different from them in that I want to also focus on being present for Claire, whereas my parents were always traveling, speaking, and educating. Their activities were impressive, but they kind of forgot about me and my sister when they were off doing their thing.

I am committed to being involved in our community and being politically active, but I also want to make time for Claire, which is why I haven't taken on all the commitments that I could have this past year. I am glad that my parents taught me the importance of being aware and involved with what's going on in the world, but I want to balance that with being a dad and a husband.

Questions:

- Do you think I'm like my parents?
- Do you think that I am doing a good job balancing fatherhood and everything else?

Love,

Jonah

Dear Jonah,

I feel resentful writing this e-mail, because it brings up feelings about my parents and the way they treated me like, basically, a trained monkey. My major differences from them are that I don't obsess over my image, I don't care about materialistic displays, and I didn't marry a man just because of his income. When I think about similarities with them, the only one I can think of is that we both value education.

I am glad I learned from my childhood that kids need more than presents and lessons and vacations to feel loved. I hope that I am able to be fully present for Claire, emotionally and physically.

Questions:

- Do you think Claire will want more materialistic things just because we are committed to not overloaded her with them?

- What similarities do you share with your parents?

XO,

Lorrie

CHAPTER 10

Requests for Change

With all that you have learned about yourself and your partner, now is a great time to express specific requests for change. You will be guided through revisiting areas that we have already discussed and will be shown how to express a request for your partner to change without being aggressive or disparaging. In the next chapter, your partner can decide which of your requests will be the focus of their commitment to change. This chapter is helpful both to those who find it difficult to ask for what they want or need in an assertive and positive way and to those who have previously avoided or deflected their partners' requests for change.

43 What I'd Like Us to Do More Of

Here is a chance to express which activities you wish that you and your partner would integrate into your life more frequently. This is not the time to ask for brand new activities; that will come later. People often make these requests, but they don't outline what exactly would change in their feelings and their overall relationship if the requested behavioral changes were made. If you show this bigger picture to your partner, the likelihood of him changing is much greater.

Use the first prompt, as well as at least three others, and end with two or three open-ended questions!

- Writing to you about this topic makes me feel _____.

- Three things I would like us to do more of are _____.

- If each of these things became a larger part of our life, I would feel _____.

- Here is how I believe that our relationship would change if we did these things more frequently: _____.

- Here is the connection between my early life and upbringing and why these activities are so important to me: _____.

- I (or you) could facilitate us doing more of these activities by _____.

- I think these activities would be hard for you, because _____.

- I would try to make these activities easier for you by _____.

Dear Alex,

This is an easy e-mail for me to write, because we've talked about this stuff. I want us to visit my family in Florida more often, I want us to hang out with my sister more, and I want you to take more time off work.

It is important to me to see my family more, because, when I was growing up, hanging out with family was always a huge part of our lives. We saw my cousins every week, and my mom spoke to her family on the phone all the time. I know my parents were rude to you when we first started dating. They have since changed their tune, and they've accepted the fact that you aren't Jewish and that we are going to raise our kids both Catholic and Jewish. (And even if they haven't really accepted it, they say that they have, and they aren't going to get in your face about it anymore.) I can facilitate us spending more time with my parents by making sure that they know that I won't tolerate any rude or passive-aggressive comments. Regarding my sister, I can have the same type of conversations with her, and I can make sure we don't hang out with her when she's in "party mode."

Questions:

- Do you think you will ever forgive my family for being mean during the first year we were together?
- Are there other ways I could make it easier for you to visit them?

All my love,

Mara

Dear Mara,

I don't feel great about writing you this e-mail, because I don't want us to fight. But if I had to pick three changes, they would be for us to talk about finances more, to have more sex, and for us to start running together more. The money one is key.

As you know, my parents were horrible at managing money and never talked about money openly. I taught myself everything I know about finances, and it makes me feel really anxious when we have no set budget. I know that you don't mean to lose sight of your spending, but I feel that you buy things on impulse and hide them. We can't keep spending like you still have your old job. If we're planning for you to stay home with kids one day, we have to focus on saving.

I realize I am anxious about this topic, and I will try to act calmer. I know that budgeting and talking about spending is strange for you, since you never had to worry about money growing up. But I want to be able to talk about money without it turning into a huge argument. That would make me feel better about everything else.

Questions:

- If we scheduled one day each month to sit down and budget for the next month, would that make anything better?

- I know I asked you this before, but if you stopped using the credit card and just used cash, would that make it easier to stay within our limits?

- Do you still get cash from your parents? You know how I feel about that, but I would rather know.

Love,

Alex

44 What I'd Like Us to Do Less Of

Here is a chance to tell your partner what you want to spend less time and energy on in your relationship. *Fighting* is the topic most often picked for this e-mail, but there are many other unproductive uses of time. Make sure to stay open and uncritical and to use "I" statements, or the e-mail may hurt your partner's feelings.

Use the first prompt, as well as at least three others, and end with two or three open-ended questions!

- Writing to you about this topic makes me feel _____.

- Three things I would like us to do less of are _____.

- If each of these things became a smaller part of our life, I would feel _____.

- Here is how I believe that our relationship would change if we did these things less frequently: _____.

- Here is the connection between my early life and upbringing and why I want to do less of these activities: _____.

- I never brought this up before (or I rarely bring this up) because _____.

- You (or I) could facilitate us doing less of these activities by _____.

- I think we started to do these activities too much when _____.

- With the time we would save, I would like to _____.

Dear Lexie,

I feel awkward writing to you about this, because I'm going to be honest with you about something I've never told you. Before, I felt scared that you would get mad, but I think we are at a better place in our relationship now. I don't actually have three things, but my one thing is big enough to count as three.

I want us to spend less time with Elizabeth. I know she is your best friend, but the reality is, she's also your ex. When we first started dating, I thought we would gradually spend less time with her as we got more serious. That didn't happen. I don't like the fact that she spends all the holidays with us. My parents have asked why she's always around, and I say she's your best friend. But honestly, why doesn't she ever visit her family or friends on major occasions?

I like Elizabeth, but only in small doses. I want to see her once a week—max. Once every couple of weeks would be ideal. When I get home, I want to hang out with just you, not you and her. I also think she intentionally drinks too much so she needs to wait here longer before driving home. That's how it ends up with me going upstairs without you at ten at night. We could be cuddling together or talking, but instead, I am asleep, and you're with her.

I think I would feel more secure and relaxed in our relationship and in our home if Elizabeth acted more like a friend or a guest and not like a roommate.

Questions:

- Are you mad?

- Do you think this change would be possible?

I love you,

Maggie

Dear Maggie,

I feel confident writing this e-mail to you, because you are great about responding to my needs and because I think you'll be on the same page with all of these things. My list of activities to decrease is eating out, watching TV, and shopping online.

I want to think about next steps for us, as we've discussed. We aren't getting any younger, and having kids is on the horizon. But we need to get our finances in check . I think we should stop eating out all the time, which could save us at least $200 a week. Same with the online shopping (I'm guilty of most of that).

Watching TV is nice and all, but it doesn't count as quality time in my book. Instead, we could be exercising or even playing Boggle. I miss hanging out with you without the TV, and if we're going to have kids, I don't want us to be like my family. When I was little, the only family time we had was in front of some dumb sitcom. I think between cooking more and watching TV less, we could really become a lot healthier in addition to feeling closer.

I could facilitate these changes by planning meals and by reading newspapers online instead of unwinding by shopping on Amazon or Zappos. You could facilitate these changes by not getting obsessed with any new TV series and suckering me into watching them (even though I am not too hard to convince).

Questions:

· What do you think of these suggestions?

· Did you guys watch TV growing up as much as we did, or did you have other kinds of family time?

XO,

Lexie

45 What I Want to Add to Our Relationship Right Now

Now we will turn to potential new additions to the relationship. We're talking about activities, behaviors, and ways of living. This is a harder e-mail to write, because it may feel threatening. After all, saying you want to add something entirely new to the relationship could be interpreted to mean that you don't find your partner, relationship, or life fulfilling as is. But if framed collaboratively, this is a great opportunity to give your partner concrete suggestions for positive change. Dig deep, and think about the significance of these potential changes, given your personal upbringing and the history of your relationship. This will give you the best chance of motivating your partner to incorporate your new and possibly intimidating suggestions.

Use the first prompt, as well as at least three others, and end with two or three open-ended questions!

- Writing to you about this topic makes me feel _____.

- Three things I would like us to add to our relationship are _____.

- If each of these things became part of our lives, I would feel _____.

- Here is how I believe that our relationship would change if we did these things: _____.

- Here is the connection between my early life and upbringing and why I want to do these things: _____.

- I never brought this up before (or rarely bring this up) because _____.

- You (or I) could facilitate us doing these activities by _____.

- I have not done these activities with anyone else, which means _____.

- I understand these activities may be difficult for you (or us) because _____.

- If you tried hard to do these activities, I would feel _____.

Dear Jacob,

I am shy about writing you this e-mail, because I don't like to ask for anything from you. In fact, I worked on this e-mail with my therapist, because otherwise I don't think I would be able to say much except "I can't think of anything! Things are great!" So here are two things (baby steps) I came up with that I would like us to add to our relationship.

First, I would like us to talk more during the day. I understand that work is busy, but when we go eight hours without speaking, it is hard for me to feel close. Even if it's just texting or e-mailing, hearing from you makes my day much brighter.

Second, I would like us to discuss moving forward in this relationship. I know you don't want kids—and, don't worry, I still don't either—but I think our marriage discussion was put on hold after we determined that we both want to be child-free. To me, this never meant that we would be marriage-free, so I want us to put this back on the table as something to talk about.

As for the impact of my childhood on these desires, my dad and mom would always check in with each other by phone once per day when he was at work, and she was always happy to hear from him. Also, the marriage thing is important to me because I felt that my parents had an overall good marriage, and I always envisioned the same for me. I think that a wedding would really make us feel more committed, and I would love to have that special day with you, celebrating our love.

Questions:

- Was the marriage question just set aside temporarily, or was it something that you thought we had decided against?

- Do you think that you would feel resentful having to talk to me when things were busy at work?

> All my love, always,
>
> Angie

Dear Angie,

I feel kind of bad writing about this stuff, because I think you're going to take my three things as criticism. I've mentioned them before, but lately I have stopped pursuing them, possibly out of hopelessness. But since we've been working so hard on the relationship, and I have been trying to e-mail so much (even though you know it's not my thing), I'm hoping that you'll consider my points without getting angry.

Here goes: I would like us to be able to fly, I would like you to resume driving, and I would like you to see a psychiatrist in addition to your therapist. I understand that your anxiety is bad, and that these things are difficult for you. But honestly, I can't be in a long-term relationship in which so many things are off the table because of your anxiety. It is important to me for you to work hard on these things, and it would make me feel much happier and more valued if you gave these things a genuine effort.

Also—and this is a new connection I've made—I think these things are important to me because when I was little, my mother was always stopping us from doing things because she was too nervous. She didn't let me play football because I would get a concussion, and she didn't like my dad going on long fishing trips because, as she always said, "something might happen." When you refuse to get on a plane or to try medication, I get really angry. I don't want to end up like my dad, constrained by his wife's anxiety. My mom was never diagnosed, but in retrospect, I bet she had panic disorder and generalized anxiety like you.

It would mean a lot to me if you'd see about medication and really worked on driving and flying with a therapist. I know you like your therapist, and she's great for giving you support, but from what I've been reading online, it seems that behavioral therapy and meds might really change things. Then we could fly to Paris like we always used to talk about doing.

Questions:

- How could I help? I would be willing to go to the psychiatrist with you, look up other therapists—anything.

- Did your parents acknowledge that not flying was because they were anxious or was it just normal for them?

Love,

Jacob

CHAPTER 11

The Future and Commitments to Change

In this chapter, you will be guided through sharing specific dreams for your life together—what you are looking forward to for today, tomorrow, and the rest of your lives. Based on all the work we have done thus far and all you have learned about your partner's desires, insecurities, and hopes, you may decide to commit to some meaningful life changes.

46 What I Have Learned from Writing These E-mails

You and your partner have divulged deep and personal information through these e-mail assignments. It is difficult to put yourself in a vulnerable place with someone else, even (or especially!) a partner in an intimate relationship. Recognize your partner's hard work by telling him that you've truly heard what he's been saying.

This would be a wonderful time to reread all of your partner's e-mails, so you're sure that you're not forgetting something meaningful that you'd want to mention.

Use the first prompt, as well as at least three others, and end with two or three open-ended questions!

- Writing this e-mail to you makes me feel _____.

- When I think back to all the e-mails we have written, I feel _____.

- When I think about all the hard work we have done for this relationship, I feel _____.

- Here is the e-mail that made me feel most

  · surprised: _____.

  · close to you: _____.

  · happy: _____.

  · moved: _____.

- When you make yourself vulnerable to me, I feel _____.

- When I think about everything you have shared, I feel _____.

- The hardest thing for me to tell you was _____.

- I am still worried about how you feel about me telling you _____.

- I never thought you (or I or we) would write all this e-mails, and now I feel _____.

- I am thankful that you took this book seriously, because _____.

Dear Patrick,

I feel so happy writing you this e-mail. I learned so much about you from the ten e-mails we have written. I love finding out new things about you. My favorite e-mails were those in which you discussed your childhood and your relationship with Robert. I never knew much about you as a kid, and it made me feel close to you to hear details about your life and your thoughts about your mom. I also liked hearing about you and Robert. It is a turn-on to know what you were thinking when you had sex for the first time. It was surprising that you remembered that much about it. My first experiences were all when I was much older, so I can live vicariously through you.

    When you make yourself vulnerable to me, I feel so happy and warm. I feel more optimistic about our future; I feel that we are truly on the same team. I didn't think you'd take this book seriously, and I am happy that you did, and that you got outside your comfort zone and wrote all these e-mails during work. I love you.

Love,

Adam

Dear Adam,

I feel proud writing you this e-mail, because I honestly didn't think I would be able to commit to writing ten e-mails. As you know, this isn't my wheelhouse. I am more of a strong, silent type, as you say, right?

   I felt closest to you when you told me about your dad and his drinking. I didn't really know the details of that time in your life. It impressed me how you've succeeded despite your difficult childhood, and it makes me understand why my drinking can trigger you.

   The hardest thing for me to tell you was about my mom's depression. I am used to hiding that aspect of my life, but the way you responded was warm and supportive, as usual. I am glad that we're together and that I can confide in someone for the first time.

                    Love,

                    Patrick

47 Small Ways I Could Change for Our Relationship

Now is your chance to show your partner how important she is to you and how much you genuinely care about your relationship. I firmly believe that, in a majority of cases, it only takes one partner to change a relationship—or at least start the process of change. However, if you're changing just so your partner feels forced to respond in kind, you're allowing your marriage to turn into a business transaction. Instead, try to focus on your love for your partner and your desire to make her feel secure and loved.

In this e-mail, you'll discuss three small ways that you could change. By "small," I mean things that would be difficult for you to do but would not feel impossible. You're pushing the boundaries of your comfort zone a bit, but not busting through them completely. These changes are all subjective; it doesn't matter if they feel meaningful to anyone but you and your partner. Make sure that your chosen ways to change are in line with requests that your partner has verbalized, either in earlier e-mails or throughout your life together. Refer back to chapter 3 on love languages and reread your partner's e-mails from that chapter.

Remember, if you pick a way to change that isn't in your partner's love language, it is not a true expression of love. For example, you could commit to doing 100 percent of the housework forever, which some partners would consider a mind-blowingly huge change, but if your partner genuinely doesn't care about housework, and his love language is physical touch, then your change will be viewed as disingenuous and meaningless.

Use the first prompt, as well as at least three others, and end with two or three open-ended questions!

- Writing to you about this topic makes me feel _____.

- Three small ways I could change to make you feel happier in this relationship are _____.

- Making these changes would make me feel _____.

- Here is how I believe that our relationship would change if I did these things: _____.

- Here is the connection between my early life and upbringing and why it's previously been hard for me to make these changes: _____.

- I haven't changed in these ways previously because _____.

- You could make these changes easier on me by _____.

- I want to change for you (or for this relationship) because _____.

- I have not done these activities with anyone else, which means _____.

Dear Cora,

I'm excited to write you this e-mail, because finally, after all this talk, we are going to start executing some of the things we've discussed. You know me—man of action. Anyway, after rereading your e-mails, I have decided on the following three things to change.

- I'm going to call you more often during the day.
- I'm going to plan more date nights.
- I'm going to be more affectionate in public.

How do you like them apples? I think I haven't done these things before because I just didn't understand how important they were to you. My parents didn't have a touchy-feely relationship, and I never knew anything else. I got used to evading your attempts to be more affectionate, but now I think that was bad for us. I am trying to get used to being more romantic, which won't be easy. But I think if I do these things, you may feel more secure and happy with me.

Questions:

- Do you like these three things, or do you want other things?
- What kind of date nights do you want?
- Do you think you'll get bored of me if I am more emotionally available? Just kidding, but not really.

I love you,

Jonas

Dear Jonas,

I am ambivalent about writing you this e-mail, because, if I'm going to be open with you here, I feel that I have tried to change in a million ways before, and it never results in any closeness. But this time I am going to try to change in ways that would be particularly special for you, given everything you've shared with me, and I am going to do it without secretly hoping that you do anything back for me. Maybe that's the key I was missing before.

So my three things:

- I'm going to leave you alone at work and not call you so much.

- I'm going to plan more girls' nights, so you can go out with your friends without me sitting home, waiting for you and texting you.

- I'm going to grow my hair out.

I think each of these things would take me out of my comfort zone. The first is tough for me, because I really miss you during the day. But I know you find it hard to focus when I interrupt you, so it would be a big change for me that I know you'd like. The next one is hard, because I am an introvert at heart, but I know myself, and if I don't have anything to do, then I will resent you going out with your friends while I'm home alone. So I will take your suggestion and plan stuff during your poker nights and when you go to happy hour. But it would help me stick to these two if you texted me so I know you're there if I need you.

The last one is something I never did for another partner— change my looks for them. My mom always told me never to change for any guy, but hey, look where that advice got her.

Maybe I shouldn't have listened. I know you're always making subtle (not really) remarks about how good my hair looked long, so I am going outside my comfort zone and changing just for you.

Questions:

- Which of these means the most to you?
- Are you going to get mad if I call sometimes anyway?

XO,

Cora

48 Big Ways I Could Change for Our Relationship

It's time to go big or go home! The previous e-mail warmed you up to the idea of making concrete changes for the good of your relationship, and hopefully you received positive feedback from your partner for trying to change in those ways. You probably also feel good about yourself for pushing outside of your comfort zone and genuinely trying to change for the better. Many people did not grow up seeing their parents make major efforts to change for one another, and you can break that pattern now. It is difficult to objectively assess your own contribution to the difficulties in your relationship, push past your defenses ("it's not me—it's you!"), and commit to change. This e-mail could be the game changer in your relationship.

Even if your partner's response to the small changes you committed to in the last e-mail was more tepid than you'd envisioned, don't lose hope. Some relationships have deeper issues which can't be fully addressed by small changes. In those cases, it may be necessary to make major changes to catapult your relationship to a new and closer level. As in the prior chapter, don't worry about what "big" would mean to anyone but you and your partner. It is subjective and based on your unique experiences, feelings, and relationship.

In this e-mail, you'll be discussing three big ways in which you could single-handedly change the landscape of your relationship. You have learned so much about your partner by now, including her background and her deepest needs and desires. You can use this information to make a large-scale effort to improve your dynamic.

Use the first prompt, as well as at least three others, and end with two or three open-ended questions!

- Writing to you about this topic makes me feel _____.

- Three major ways I could change to make you feel happier in this relationship are _____.

- Making these changes would make me feel _____.

- Here is how I believe that our relationship would change if I did these things: _____.

- Here is the connection between my early life and upbringing and why it's previously been hard for me to make these changes: _____.

- I haven't changed in these ways before now because _____.

- You could make these changes easier on me by _____.

- I want to change for you (or for this relationship) because _____.

- I have not done these activities with anyone else, which means _____.

Dear Kate,

I feel sad writing you this e-mail, because I think I should have already done the things I am now going to commit to doing. But better late and never, right? I think I have finally realized that I have been selfish. My changes: I'm going to call if I'm going to be late from work, I'm going to talk to Mom about not dropping by randomly, and I'm not going to get on you about finding a job.

All of these have been tremendous stressors in our lives, and, honestly, I have not acted nicely about them. Here is what I have realized.

- My dad never called my mom if he was going to be coming home late, so that became normal for me. I have realized that this isn't fair, and I don't want Sean and Tyler to treat their wives like this when they grow up.

- I know Mom is lonely now that Dad isn't around, and that's why I have shied away from asking her to call before stopping by. But you've always been good to her, and I should respect your feelings, so I'll talk to her about it this week.

- I have been annoying you about going back to work now that Tyler is in pre-K, and I think this comes from watching my parents. Mom went back to work when I was three, but I was over at the neighbor's a lot, and I know this isn't what we want for the boys. If you want to stay home, we can make it work.

These would be big changes for me, but I am willing to do them to make this marriage stronger. Talking about divorce was the rock-bottom point of my life. I am willing to change in whatever way necessary so we don't get back to that place.

Questions:

- Which of these changes is most important to you?
- Do you like how I am digging deep and discussing my family like you always want me to do?

I love you,

Zack

Dear Zack,

I am hopeful about writing you this e-mail. I see all the changes you've made in recent months, and I am ready to try to change myself.

I am going to have sex with you more often, and I am also going off the pill. I have read about the pill lowering your sex drive, and it bothers me that I don't feel in the mood anymore. I know your love language is touch, and I recognize how important sex is to you—and to our marriage.

I am going to figure out what I want to do for a career. I understand that you are worried about our finances with me at home, even though T is in pre-K. I have kept this a secret for a week now, but I spoke with Molly about going back to the office twenty hours a week. I just had this idea of me staying home like my mom did, but it doesn't make sense for us and our finances. This was a tough decision for me, but I think you were right, and I think working will be a good thing for me.

I am also going to plan some more date nights. Most of my friends are okay leaving the kids with sitters at this point. Maybe it's just because my mom and dad so rarely went out at night. But I think a sitter would be okay if it meant we were happier in front of the boys the rest of the time.

I hope that if I make these changes, we will keep the connection going that we have rebuilt over the past few months.

My questions:

- What do you think about the part-time work option?

- What do you think about me going off the pill? That would mean condoms for a while, until we decide about baby number three.

I love you,

Kate

49 The Awards Ceremony!

By the time you write this e-mail, you and your partner have likely implemented some of the big and small changes you committed to in e-mails 47 and 48. Recognize this gift that you have given to each other by expressing your appreciation and gratitude! Gratitude is a positive and healthy emotion and is associated with happiness; expressing it openly is beneficial for your relationship.

This e-mail is like an awards ceremony for the work you have done so far, so don't hold back on the pomp and circumstance. No amount of positive feedback is excessive; this is the time to ramp up your expressions of love. Show your partner that her efforts are changing your perspective about your relationship. Also, don't hold back in expressing your pride about your own efforts to change. By this point in the book, you and your partner have both shown tremendous commitment to your relationship and to each other. How romantic! And how impressive!

This time, use all the prompts to craft your e-mail to each other.

- Writing you this e-mail makes me feel _____.

- You really impressed or surprised me by changing in these ways: _____.

- I really impressed or surprised myself by changing in these ways: _____.

- I am grateful to you for _____.

- I am grateful to myself for _____.

- Here is how I feel about you as a partner: _____.

- This is how I feel about our relationship right now: _____.

- All of our changes have made me feel this way about our future: _____.

No questions needed, unless you want to!

Dear Jason,

Writing you this e-mail, I feel very loving toward you. You've really impressed me with all things you have done, but the most impressive was the way you have totally done an about-face about sex. I used to be scared to go to bed at the same time as you, because you wouldn't take no for an answer, even if I was exhausted. Now, I love going upstairs with you, because you are so much more laid back. I have been able to get excited about snuggling with you and kissing you, since I know it doesn't always have to lead to sex, and I think we have been having sex even more than we used to.

Another big change was that you have really stuck to this e-mail thing. I was shocked that you sent me your e-mails even before I sent you mine. I would have bet money that I would have ended up nagging you to write to me. So that made me feel awesome; I feel that you're really recommitting to me

I impressed myself by inviting your mom over for lunch twice since you said that you would really like me to do that. I surprised myself by not hating it. It is different for me to hang out with her if I know that it is something good I am doing for the marriage.

I feel happy about our relationship right now, and I feel that you're really a great partner. I am grateful that we are together and that we have weathered all of our issues and are stronger for it.

Love,

Mina

Dear Mina,

I am writing you this with a big smile on my face. I think we have done lots of great work together over the past few months. The biggest change you made was in your attitude toward sex. As soon as I laid off a little, you started initiating and even trying new things. I was surprised, to say the least. You are so hot.

Another awesome thing you've done is go back to therapy for your anxiety. I am so proud of you for tackling that head-on. I hope it was for yourself, as well as for me, but either way, I am glad and grateful that you started going again. I have already seen changes in your outlook and the number of things you're willing to do outside the house.

I think you're a wonderful wife, and you will always be the girl of my dreams. I love you, sweetheart, and I will love growing old with you.

Your loving husband,

Jason

CHAPTER 12

What Next?

Hopefully all the hard work you put in—writing these often-difficult e-mails and mindfully responding to your partner's—has been helpful for your relationship. You are likely feeling closer and more connected, with a new understanding of your partner's inner workings and background. Your intimate life is probably much improved as well. Now the question is whether you can maintain this new connection.

Many couples want to continue e-mailing each other after they have completed the exercises in this book, because they want to maintain the intimate connection that they have built. Other couples want to move forward to verbal conversations instead. Still others want to combine e-mail and verbal conversations, and this will likely lead to the greatest level of connection. The following e-mails will allow you and your partner to discuss how you'd like to move forward.

50 Keep On E-mailing?

If you've discovered a new love for writing e-mails to your partner, this would be a great time to commit to continuing the practice. This can be your special secret activity as a couple, the thing that helps keep you feeling connected and close even in times of stress. These e-mails can revisit some of the topics in this book, since nobody will have answered all the prompts, or they can be brand new, created by you or your partner (or the two of you together). Committing to continued e-mailing is a wonderful way to reassure the more verbally expressive partner that you will continue to discuss deep and meaningful topics even though you've come to the end of this book.

Use the first prompt, as well as at least three others, and end with two or three open-ended questions!

- Discussing continuing e-mailing makes me feel _____.

- I would (or would not) like to keep e-mail as part of our regular communication, because _____.

- Writing (or reading) these e-mails has made me feel _____.

- If we e-mail, I'd like it to be this often: _____.

- My concerns about continuing e-mailing are _____.

Dear Irene,

I feel positive writing this, because I really liked writing these e-mails. I have felt like we have learned a lot about each other, and the e-mails didn't turn into fights like I feared they might. Writing to you has helped me reflect about my upbringing, which has helped me think more about my own parenting now. Reading your e-mails made me realize that you are still the complex, interesting person I fell in love with, and I want to keep learning about you every day. If we keep e-mailing, I want it to be on a spontaneous basis, but at least every couple of weeks. My only concern would be that you might be upset if I don't e-mail frequently enough, so I wouldn't want a set weekly assignment anymore.

Questions:

- What do you think about continuing e-mailing?
- What did you like best about e-mailing over the past three months?

I love you,

Morris

Dear Morris,

I feel good writing to you about this topic, because I was getting anxious about our communication falling off once the book was over. I would really enjoy continuing to communicate via e-mail, even if it's not as frequently. I have loved reading about how you grew up and your thoughts about your life and our life together. I want to continue feeling as close as I do now.

- How often would you want to e-mail?
- Do you think we can talk about these types of topics more often even if we don't e-mail as much?

Kisses,

Irene

51 Did We Miss Something?

No book can fully capture the unique experiences and histories of every couple who reads it. This e-mail focuses on the issues that you feel were left out of your correspondence. There is a list of possible topics as a starting point, but please think deeply about other potential topics for later e-mails or in-person discussions.

In this e-mail, the goal is only to list topics that you may want to be included in future discussions. However, if you feel like it would be useful to discuss these topics in a subsequent e-mail, feel free! After all, you are skilled enough at e-mail correspondence by now to figure out your own prompts and to communicate respectfully and productively. You can also print the list of other potential topics at http://www.newhar binger.com/34602 so you can cross them out as you go through them.

Use the first prompt, as well as at least three others, and end with two or three open-ended questions!

- Here's how I feel about writing to you about topics we may have missed: _____.

- Here are two or three topics that I would like to discuss in the future:

  - politics (our differences and changes in our point-of-view over time)

  - religion

- health
- infertility
- my relationship with your family
- your relationship with my family
- step-parenting
- adoption
- career changes
- retirement planning
- the use of technology and the amount of computer time, smartphone time, and screen time in our home
- sleeping in separate beds (due to snoring, discomfort, or other non-emotional issues)
- having family live with us
- houseguests
- vacations
- buying a second home or other major investments
- estate planning
- giving money to adult children
- giving money to grandchildren

- how often we care for grandchildren
- drastic changes in appearance, such as plastic surgery
- throwing a large party or other event
- environmental issues
- community involvement
- alcohol or recreational drug use
- the friends we spend time with

- For me, the most important/interesting topic from this list is _____.

- Talking about this topic would make me feel _____.

- The major points I want us to discuss about this topic are _____.

- I am (or am not) anxious bringing up these topics with you, because _____.

- Here's how I feel about seeing what topics you bring up: _____.

- I would rather discuss these topics via e-mail (or in person), because _____.

Dear Karen,

I feel hesitant writing to you about other topics we could discuss, because we were doing so well, and I don't want to add anything that might make us fight. Just in terms of what would be interesting to me, I would pick how I feel about your increasing involvement in the temple, and whom we spend time with. I might want to talk about these topics via e-mail at first, but if you want to discuss them in person, that's fine too.

- Do you think we can talk about these issues without fighting?
- What are yours?

Thanks for reading,

Joe

Dear Joe,

I am excited to write to you about other topics we could discuss, because some important ones were left out. One is houseguests, because of recent events, when we were very much not on the same page about how long they should stay, among other issues. I also want to discuss our long-standing plan of a summer home, because I have had a change of heart recently, given how much of a pain summer homes seem to be for others to maintain. Lastly, I want to discuss estate planning, because I should know more of what you've been doing with our savings. I am embarrassed that I have delegated that entirely to you.

- Which of these are you most interested in discussing?
- Are you going to be mad if I don't really want a beach house?

Love,

Karen

52 ❤ What If You're Still Not Okay?

Some couples will realize through this process that they still have a long way to go to attain the intimacy that they desire. Couples counseling may be a good idea to help you get there. All of the honest sharing that you've done via e-mail will allow you to start the counseling process at a much deeper level than couples who have not discussed their issues openly. If you have written e-mails to one another about areas of continued conflict, you can also show them to your clinician so he or she can more fully understand your dynamic. While couples counseling may be necessary to get to the next level in your relationship, both partners first need to be on the same page to start this process.

If you feel satisfied with your relationship, there is no need to write this e-mail unless you and your partner would like to explore your feelings about possibly engaging in couples counseling in the future. Similarly, if you already are in counseling, you can skip this e-mail, unless you want to reevaluate whether you find it useful.

Use the first prompt, as well as at least three others, and end with two or three open-ended questions!

- Writing to you about the idea of couples counseling makes me feel _____.

- When I think about us going into counseling, I feel _____.

- Here is what I have heard about couples counseling: _____.

- Here is what I thought about couples counseling when we (or I) tried it before: _____.

- I think we need (or do not need) counseling to help us grow even closer, because _____.

- Here is what we've worked on already and what we would need to work on in counseling: _____.

- In the future, I would (or would not) be open to the idea of counseling, because _____.

Dear Anne,

I feel wary writing this e-mail. I don't think we need counseling, but I know you were pushing for it for a while, so maybe I will consider it. I feel closer now after doing these e-mails, but I think you still are unhappy with me sometimes. We've worked on our communication, but there is always room for improvement. I am open to the idea of counseling if things don't improve after the kids go back to school, when our schedules aren't so crazy.

Questions:

- Do you still think we need counseling?
- How much closer do you feel now versus last year?

Love,

Marty

Dear Marty,

I am happy writing you this e-mail, because for the first time in a while, I don't think we need couples counseling. I have enjoyed writing these e-mails and connecting more. I have realized that I have some childhood issues to work through, so I think that I am going to start individual counseling at some point soon. If the need arises for us to go to couples counseling in the future, though, I hope you will be willing.

My questions:

- Are you surprised I don't think we need counseling anymore?
- Would you be open to going in the future?

I love you,

Anne

CHAPTER 13

Transitioning to Conversations

This book would not be complete without a brief discussion of how to transition from e-mails to in-person conversations. Many couples may fear that they may revert to attacks, withdrawal, mockery, or other toxic patterns when resuming face-to-face discussions of difficult or emotional topics. Fortunately, there are some rules that can decrease the likelihood of veering into dangerous territory. Many of them will be familiar, as they are the same rules you observed when e-mailing. A printable, bullet-pointed version of these rules appears at http://www.newharbinger.com/34602, which you can use during your first in-depth, in-person conversations.

When talking face to face about sensitive topics, discussions can escalate quickly, particularly if either partner feels triggered by a certain subject. To limit partners' volatility and stress levels, try to schedule important discussions for times when both partners feel relaxed. If this is at opposite times for each partner, try to compromise, or be creative. Putting your children in front of the television for a half hour while you talk in the other room is not the end of the world. In fact, if it allows you to feel closer and happier—which, in turn, affects how you relate to your kids—this half hour of screen time may be the best thing you did as a parent all day! Additionally, phone calls should not be overlooked as a way for partners to bond. If partners can talk during their commute or a work break, this dead time can be transformed into a gift for your relationship.

When sitting down for a discussion, sit near each other, rather than across the room, so you can make eye contact and reach out to each other physically if you feel particularly close. However, be respectful of your partner's individual preferences. Some people find it difficult to make eye contact or be touched by a partner when discussing intimate or emotional issues, as the interaction then becomes overly intense, even to the point of discomfort.

Just as when you were e-mailing, avoid interrupting or rushing to respond. Some couples find it useful to alternate *speaker* and *listener* roles. Ideally, one partner, the speaker, talks for a few minutes about a topic of his choosing, while the other listens without interrupting, either verbally or nonverbally (e.g., by sighing). When the speaker is finished, the listener can ask questions or respond with her thoughts and feelings about what was just said. The speaker can then answer these questions and respond to the listener's thoughts. After one speaking-listening exchange, the partners switch roles. The second speaker can expand on the first speaker's topic or can introduce a new topic entirely.

For example, the first partner might start with, "I'd like to talk about my parents' visit this Saturday," and speak for two or three minutes about his thoughts, feelings, concerns, or hopes. The second partner listens, and when he is done speaking, she responds, "I am actually pretty worried about the visit too. How come you're so anxious this time? I didn't know you were that affected by their comments." The first partner may respond with a discussion of why his mother's comments about his job have bothered him more recently. Then it's the second partner's turn, and she may decide to keep talking about the upcoming visit, or to talk about something else, like her job stress.

Be careful when you ask questions. While they can be wonderful indicators of genuine interest and engagement, they also can lead to disengagement and defensiveness, if one partner feels interrogated or overwhelmed by a barrage of fact-finding questions. For instance, if your partner says she is wondering what it would be like to explore a different religion, don't ask, "When did you think this? Was it during the sermon? Why didn't you tell me sooner?" Instead, try expressing your feelings first and then asking a more open-ended question, one that will give you the bigger picture without pinning her down on specifics, like, "I am surprised to hear that. What's leading to your curiosity?"

Questions that target deeper thoughts, feelings, motivations, and experiences (questions that often begin with *why* or *how*) are more productive than questions about specifics (which tend to start with *what*, *when*, or *where*), which lead to tangents. Deeper, noncombative questions will help your partner feel secure about confiding in you and will increase her likelihood of confiding more in the future.

The same rules of "niceness" apply when talking face-to-face, perhaps even more than when e-mailing. This means that you must not attack, criticize, engage in name-calling, or mock your partner. When discussing behavior, use the same neutral language that was suggested for e-mails—speak as if you were describing what you saw in a video (e.g., say "when you looked away," not "when you ignored me"). Also, especially when meeting in person, many people hide behind sarcasm or jokes when feeling exposed or insecure. While this is understandable as a coping mechanism, it generally prevents people from connecting in a meaningful way within an intimate relationship.

Lastly, try to be open and vulnerable and to examine your own contribution to any relationship conflict. If you use conversations to push a certain agenda or to find fault in your partner, they will likely devolve into arguments quickly. Instead, accept responsibility for anything you did to make a situation more difficult or stressful. This is the surest way to show your partner that you are committed to your relationship and are not just trying to save face. The more honest engagement and enthusiasm you bring to your conversations, the better you will feel about your relationship as a whole.

Emotional Check-ins

If you would like to stick to the same schedule of weekly intimate communication, it can be useful to schedule an "emotional check-in" once a week. This ensures that you make time to talk about topics aside from quotidian household matters, just as when you were e-mailing. An emotional check-in should last no more than twenty or thirty minutes, which is enough to make the more verbally expressive partner feel connected, but not so long that the less verbally expressive partner feels overwhelmed. These check-ins are an excellent way to counteract couples' tendency to revert to small talk and superficial conversations that can be coasted through.

During these check-ins, each partner uses "I feel" statements to discuss the current state of the relationship. For example, "I feel that we've been pretty close lately" or "I feel resentful lately." Try to stick to current issues; don't use the check-in as a jumping-off point to revisit longstanding grudges. Use the same tips for positive communication that were covered earlier in this chapter.

You can use emotional check-ins to discuss any topic from this book, the topics from e-mail 51, or other subjects that help you learn more about each other's background, thoughts, or feelings. New issues crop up all the time, based on what's going on in the world, interactions with friends, family members, and coworkers, as well as your own personal reflections. If either partner goes to therapy, the topics discussed in session can also be excellent conversation-starters.

Conclusion

Congratulations on finishing this book! Most couples will end this process with a greater understanding of themselves, their partners, and their relationship, which will hopefully lead to renewed feelings of closeness, intimacy, and love. If this is true for you, why not celebrate or honor all the work that you have done together? Printing your e-mails and binding them into a book would be a great way to memorialize the work you've done, and this allows you both to reread the e-mails at your leisure. Some couples enjoy creating a ritual out of it, reading the book or certain e-mails together on special occasions, like anniversaries. Even if you don't print the e-mails, you can share which e-mails were most meaningful to you, both to write and to receive, and reread these privately.

A relationship is a journey, and over a lifetime with your partner, your individual identities and your dynamic as a couple are bound to develop and change. A relationship is fluid and goes through many phases, as well as many ups and downs. Turn to this book again in a year, in a few years, or whenever stress and conflict arise. The e-mails can guide you again and again through discussing difficult topics with open-ness, mindfulness, love, and sensitivity.

As you may have experienced, many relationships grow more distant over time, and they can only remain strong with explicit efforts to maintain connection. Take responsibility for your own happiness and do everything you can to be open, vulnerable, and loving with your partner. The work you have done and the communication tools you have learned will allow your relationship to weather tough times more easily and to remain connected and close in the face of setbacks. Good luck, and keep e-mailing!

References

1. Gottman, J. M., and J. DeClaire. *The Relationship Cure*. New York: Three Rivers Press, 2001.

2. Chapman, Gary. *The Five Love Languages: The Secret to Love That Lasts*. Chicago: Northfield Press, 2010.

3. Fogarty, Thomas F. "The Distancer and the Pursuer." In *Compendium II, The Best of the Family*. New Rochelle, NY: The Center for Family Learning, 1978–1983.

4. Hendrix, Harville. *Getting the Love You Want*. New York: Henry Holt, 1988.